ORIGINS OF ECONOMIC THOUGHT IN MODERN JAPAN

The post-war development of the Japanese economy has attained legendary status and, as such, is extremely well documented. Less well known, however, is the stream of economic thought which emerged during the Enlightenment period of Japanese history, the effects of which were to be fundamental to future economic development.

The aim of *Origins of Economic Thought in Modern Japan* is to elucidate the economic thought in the period of Japanese Enlightenment (or the first two decades of the Meiji era). At this time, although intellectuals differed about the means, there was general agreement for the need to modernize the country by abolishing all remaining aspects of feudalism and generally opening up to new and Western economic thought. The author examines the main characteristics of economic thought at this time and, in particular, the ascendancy and predominance of nationalism among proponents of both protectionism and free trade. An introductory chapter outlines the historical background, subsequent chapters examine the writing of influential figures and the establishment of economic institutions which were to play a major role in later economic development. The final chapter on the Imperial Constitution frames the historical context and marks the decline of Enlightenment and the ascendance of Imperialism.

Chuhei Sugiyama is Professor of Economics at the Tokyo Keizai University. He is an honorary member of the British Association for Japanese Studies and has written extensively on Japanese economic thought.

ORIGINS OF ECONOMIC THOUGHT IN MODERN JAPAN

Chuhei Sugiyama

ROUTLEDGE

London and New York

First published 1994
by Routledge
11 New Fetter Lane, London EC4P 4EE

Simultaneously published in the USA and Canada
by Routledge
29 West 35th Street, New York, NY 10001

Typeset in Garamond by
Ponting–Green Publishing Services,
Chesham, Buckinghamshire
Printed and bound in Great Britain by
Biddles Ltd, Guildford and King's Lynn

British Library Cataloguing in Publication Data
A catalogue record for this book is available from
the British Library

Library of Congress Cataloging in Publication Data
Sugiyama, Chuhei, 1921–
Origins of economic thought in modern Japan /
Chuhei Sugiyama.
p. cm.
Includes bibliographical references and index.
ISBN 0–415–08591–8
1. Economics–Japan–History. 2. Japan–Economic policy.
I. Title.
HB126.J2S794 1993
330.952–dc20 93–11319
CIP

ISBN 0–415–08591–8 (hbk)

CONTENTS

PREFACE

The aim of this book is to throw light on the economic thought in the period of the 'Japanese Enlightenment'[1] or the 'first two turbulent decades'[2] of the Meiji era (1868–1912), when the leading intellectuals, though disagreeing among themselves on a variety of problems, were agreed in their sincere wish to modernize their country by uprooting all remnants of feudalism and by enlightening the people. The economic thought dealt with in this book is one of the main phases of the enlightenment; thus, the book might also be entitled 'Enlightenment and Economic Thought in Japan'. The modernization or enlightenment period, when it proceeds to a certain point, must face the new realities of the world. Once a country opens itself to the outer world, it cannot help sharing world problems, if in its own way. In that sense the characteristics of economic thought as part of the enlightenment may be better grasped when placed in the wider historical context of the whole Meiji period. The first chapter looks at the historical background. The following chapters deal with the economic thought of some leading thinkers, most notably Fukuzawa Yukichi, and with some conspicuous events, namely the institutionalization of business and economic education in the modern sense, the birth of a pioneer business enterprise and the first appearance of economic journalism, all of which are deeply connected with the reception and naturalization of Western economic thought in the period. The reader will easily recognize that economic thought in that period, although to varying degrees, was inseparably fused with nationalism. In that sense this book might also be partially entitled 'Enlightenment and Nationalism'.

The turning point which symbolically marks the subsiding of enlightenment and the launching of imperialism is the promulgation of the 'Constitution of the Empire of Great Japan' in 1889. Subsequent events, such as the Sino–Japanese War of 1894–5, the colonization of Formosa which was ceded by China as a result of the war, the long wished-for revision of the so-called unequal treaties with some Western countries, the enactment of the Preservation of the Peace Act, the Russo–Japanese War of 1904–5 and the resulting possession of South Sakhalin, Kuril Islands and Port Arthur, and the colonization of Korea in 1910, exemplify the path that Japan followed thereafter. Nationalism was the bridge between enlightenment and imperialism. The last chapter of this book deals with the Constitution.

NOTE

Japanese words are transcribed according to the standard Hepburn romanization. Japanese names are given in the normal Japanese order, i.e. family name first and given name next, with the exception of those in the Notes.

ACKNOWLEDGEMENTS

Some chapters of this book, though newly rewritten, were published in original form as follows. Chapter 2, 'The Economic Thought of Nishi Amane', Chapter 3, 'The Economic Thought of Tsuda Mamichi' and Chapter 4, 'The Economic Thought of Fukuzawa Yukichi' correspond respectively to Chapter 3, 'Nishi Amane and Tsuda Mamichi' and Chapter 2, 'Fukuzawa Yukichi' of *Enlightenment and Beyond: Political Economy comes to Japan*, edited by Chuhei Sugiyama and Hiroshi Mizuta, University of Tokyo Press, 1988 (pp. 59–72, 37–57).

Chapter 5, 'The Birth of Business Education' and Chapter 9, 'The Imperial Constitution' correspond respectively to two articles, 'The Early Days of Higher Education in Japan: With Special Reference to Business Education' and 'Reflections on the Meiji Constitution', in *International Studies* (IS/89/204, 1989/II, pp. 1–12; IS/89/208, 1989/IV, pp. 12–21), Suntory Toyota International Centre for Economic and Related Disciplines, London School of Economics and Political Science.

I am grateful to those concerned who generously permitted me to rewrite these items and to publish them here. I am also grateful to Ros Ramage who has kindly taken the trouble to improve my English style.

1

THE DEVELOPMENT OF ECONOMIC THOUGHT IN MEIJI JAPAN

The aim of this chapter is to outline the development of Japanese economic thought in the era called Meiji, the era that put an end to long-lived feudalism by the Restoration of 1868. The characteristics of the age of the Japanese Enlightenment may become clearer when seen against this background.

Some people would no doubt be surprised to learn of a man like Sada Kaiseki who in the early days of Meiji era zealously asserted that 'every expedience is an evil', that 'inconvenience must be esteemed' in order to bring peace and wealth to the nation, and that railways, umbrellas, lamps, steamships and other similar innovations could only be harmful. Such an assertion, that everything convenient is an evil, was rooted in nationalistic sentiments against the then fashionable trend of Westernization. However, those who are now seriously conscious of such outcomes of so-called civilization as the noise and polluted air of big cities, the growing toll of road accidents, the horrors of atomic weapons and even of power stations and everything else of like kind might be inclined to sympathize with Sada, feeling that his attitudes cannot be totally reduced to reactionarism.

In fact, Sada merely represented the feelings of ordinary people, by no means small in number, who, accustomed to the traditional way of life under the Tokugawa feudalist regime, were either implicitly or explicitly opposed to the new government or at least unable to adapt themselves to the new way of life that made its appearance so suddenly. To Sada everything convenient was brought in from abroad and anything that was brought in from abroad seemed harmful, because he feared that innovations must lead to the impoverishment of those who lived by traditional trades and so would land the whole nation in misery. He never ceased to write and lecture on this topic, and even went as far as to petition the government to stop the importation, and to discourage the use, of any Western commodity whatsoever. However, because his influence was limited compared with that of the notorious motto of 'Civilization and Culture' which was then in fashion, and because his attitude was seen as a mere feudal reaction to what was inevitable, his was a voice crying in the wilderness.[1] Nevertheless, his opinion, regardless of whether or not he was concious of it, shared common ground with the mercantilist thought that had prevailed in the West; namely criticism, originating in the suffering of national industry, of levels of imports and of the resultant deficit in the balance of trade.

To Meiji Japan the West represented all that was modern not only in goods and institutions themselves but also in the ideas that gave birth to them. Fukuzawa Yukichi, who, as we shall see in Chapter 4, made Western civilization his hallmark of value, may be said to have represented this leading stream of thought. The Western ideas which constituted the impetus to the modernization of Japan consisted in the main of British liberalism, or utilitarianism based upon it, French notions of people's rights, German nationalism and, one might add, American sects of Christianity. These ideas were brought in almost at the same time and apparently at random by different people, but sometimes even by the same persons.

In the sphere of economic thought, however, there is no doubt that Britain played the predominant part, at least in the earlier years of the era. Within the first twenty years, Japanese translations were published of books by such authors as A. L. Perry, Francis Wayland, M. G. and Henry Fawcett, J. E. T. Rogers, F. A. Walker, T. R. Malthus, J. S. Mill, C. F. Bastiat, T. P. Thompson, Leone Levi, Augustus Mongredien, W. S. Jevons, J. E. Cairnes, Walter Bagehot, Adam Smith and H. D. Macleod. It goes without saying that all of these, regardless of their nationalities, belong more or less to the liberal school of British origin. Here again selections were at random and the order of translation was such that, for example, Perry, the American propagator of Bastiat's economic thought, was taken up before Bastiat himself, and Bastiat, the French propagator of Smithian principles, before Smith himself. Moreover, none of these translations was either complete or accurate. Yet, if one considers the short space of time which had elapsed since the Japanese had officially opened their country to the outer world in 1858,[2] this may be said to have been quite a remarkable process.

The ideas of economic liberalism, however, were not introduced soley by translations. They were also offered to the reading public by means of original writings, of which the most conspicuous authors were Kanda Takahira, Fukuzawa Yukichi, Tsuda Mamichi, Taguchi Ukichi and Amano Tameyuki. Kanda, who deserves the distinction of being the first to introduce Western economic thought in general and economic liberalism in particular (in his *No-Sho Ben* [On Agriculture and Trade, 1861] and in *Keizai Shogaku* [An Economic Handbook, 1867–8, which is in fact the Japanese translation of the Dutch edition of William Ellis's *Outlines of Social Economy*, 1846], which were published before the Meiji Restoration), declared that people are by nature different from each other. 'Some are clever while others are dull, some strive industriously but others remain lazy, some tend to be thrifty but others wasteful', so that it is only natural that those who are at the same time clever, industrious and thrifty grow rich, whereas those who are at once dull, lazy and wasteful can only become poor. Therefore to try to eliminate the inequality of property is nothing other than to rob the rich in order to give to the poor, the result of which would only be to discourage virtue and encourage vice. It would simply be a policy to impoverish the nation.[3]

This is of course the fundamental theme of classical political economy. Though stated so far in general terms, it was in fact no idle talk for Kanda, because his purpose lay in refuting the arguments of a sect of people who were opposed to the land reform that was then under discussion. These people were of the opinion that the old system of land tax based on the traditional system of ownership should not be altered, because once the free buying and selling of land was introduced, inequality of property ownership would automatically be increased. Kanda's proposition, in contrast, was to permit the freedom of buying and selling land and to replace tax in kind by a tax in cash by means of land bills to be issued by the proprietors according to the value of each piece of land. By so doing, high land prices would be lowered and low ones raised, so that an equilibrium would eventually be reached. This likewise is nothing other than the fundamental theme of *laissez-faire*. And it may be noted once again that this general theme was professed not for its own sake but as an issue vitally related to the problems of the day. The reason was that, among many other policies for removing the vestiges of the feudal system, land reform was of particular importance. Since there was hardly any industry worthy of note at that time, over 80 per cent of governmental revenue had to come from land tax. Without it, therefore, any policy of the new government could not have been carried out. Here one sees the progressive role played by economic liberalism in the earliest stages of modernization.

Political economy was in itself an unfamiliar subject to almost everyone in Japan at the beginning of the era. Consequently, there was a need for someone acquainted with political economy to popularize the subject. This was the task that Fukuzawa Yukichi, who was to be the versatile champion of the 'Japanese Enlightenment'[4] allotted to himself. As early as 1867, in one of the three volumes of the bestseller *Seiyo Jijo* (Conditions in the West), he answered the needs of the age by putting a popular economic textbook from an Edinburgh publisher into Japanese in such a plain and simple way that any literate person might follow. The text runs:

> Political economy is connected with the supply of man's physical wants, and the enlargement of the material elements of wealth and enjoyments. The first great work on political economy was named *The Wealth of Nations*. It was seen that men acquired wealth by household economy; and it was considered that the same term might be usefully applied to the goods earned by nations from a proper application of the laws of political economy. It would be an entire mistake, however, to suppose that political economy is a system for acquiring riches, or even for saving what is acquired. It is not a system for controlling men's actions, but for discovering how men are induced by their natural propensities to act.[5]

About the duties of government it concludes:

> The government cannot provide for the subsistence of the people at large; for the extent of the remuneration which workers should receive for their labour, or the extent to which they should work for the wages they obtain; for the extent to which commodities of any kind – such as food, clothing, &c. – should be procured, the manner in which they should be sold, or the price that should be paid for them: generally speaking, government should not interfere with trade.[6]

Having thus introduced the *laissez-faire* idea to the reader, Fukuzawa then proceeded to write his own book in two volumes under the title *Minkan Keizairoku* (Popular Political Economy). This was based on the same principles, but this time was written in a more systematized way although still in a popular style. The chapters, for instance, of the first volume are: industry, money, rise and fall of prices, interest, government, and taxation. The contents were nothing more than a popularized essence of the theories of classical political economy and the absence of chapters dealing with the capitalist mode of production and distribution merely corresponded to the reality of the day. In volume 2 of the book he says that the activities that should be left to the government are 'those which are useful to the nation at large such as railways, telegraph, gas and water supplies'. And yet 'it would be a great mistake to misunderstand the principle and to believe that the government may do anything in order to enrich the nation.' While thus following the *laissez-faire* principle on the one hand, he discloses his tendency to nationalism, in reference to railways, on the other. With the comparison between the advanced countries and the late-starter Japan in mind, he says:

> We are no more than crawling worms, whereas they have wings to fly with. How can we rival them with their industry and trade, with their forces and tactics? We have never been in greater danger. This is why the construction of railways is now such an immediate necessity.[7]

It may be of interest in this connection that Kato Hiroyuki, who only a few years later was to become famous as a nationalist and who remained so throughout the rest of his life, appeared at this time to be a liberal economically as well as politically. In his book *Koeki Mondo* (A Dialogue on Trade), written about the same time and for the same popularizing purpose as Fukuzawa's *Seiyo Jijo, Gaihen* (Conditions in the West, vol. 2) and perhaps with such sentiments as Sada's in mind, Kato praises the benefit of free trade just as unreservedly as did Fukuzawa, or even more so, saying that 'as there are nice things in the Western countries that are not available in Japan and there are commodities in Japan which are attractive to the Westerners, it is useful and enriching for both sides to trade freely' and that 'it is not true to claim that things Western are of no avail, because what appears to be useless now may become useful as the country grows more and more civilized'.[8]

But it was perhaps too early for a more sophisticated description of political economy to appear, and it was not until 1886 that the first one of that kind, a book by Amano Tameyuki entitled *Keizai Genron* (Principles of Political Economy), was published. However, the original manuscript had already been completed four years earlier and used by Amano in his lecture at Tokyo Senmon Gakko (Tokyo School for Special Studies), the school which was afterwards to be developed into Waseda University. Amano divided the book into three different parts, and each part again into three distinct chapters. The first part dealt with production, the second with distribution and the third with exchange. Apart from their subdivision into chapters, these evidently corresponded to the first three parts of J. S. Mill's *Principles of Political Economy* (1848), and their contents were substantially, though not literally, taken from Mill's text. For example, when Amano, on the definition of political economy, states that the aim of political economy lies in inquiring into the laws that regulate production, distribution and exchange, or that political economy is the science of wealth or goods that have value, he follows closely what Mill had to say in the first pages of his book.[9] On the other hand, in some respects Amano diverges from Mill. Mill differed from any of his predecessors in that he drew a clear line between the laws respectively regulating production and distribution; from there he proceeded to his prediction of the future development of the working classes and of socialism. Amano never goes that far. One of the reasons for this difference may be attributed to the distinction between Britain in the mid-nineteenth century where the Industrial Revolution was nearly over and Japan in the latter half of the century where it was still incipient.

Immediately after *Keizai Genron*, Amano published another book, this time concerned not with economic theory but with economic policy, or economic art as he put it. In his first book he had already urged the need to discriminate between theory and policy. Theory does and must concern factual observation which allows no room for evaluation. 'The science of political economy does not tell more than what and why. It never tells what should or should not be done. What concerns the science is the facts and the law that underlies them.'[10]

Evaluation, or the application of theory, belongs to an entirely different sphere, which is policy. That, Amano said, was why he had to write the latter book, *Shosei Hyojun* (Principles of Commercial Policy, 1886). This doctrine was essentially taken from what J. E. Cairnes had said in his work, *The Character and Logical Method of Political Economy* (1857). Beyond indicating this similarity, no further comments on the book are called for except to say that it also shows that Amano was no longer solely concerned with the popularization of political economy, but had embarked on the writing of specific studies. Furthermore, he was so little satisfied with limiting his interests merely to principles, whether of political economy as such or of economic policy, that he started a periodical in 1889 and another in 1895, both at his own expense. The former was short-lived, but the latter, which was confined purely to economic discussions, survived, a fact which suggests that political economy was now ceasing to be an unfamiliar subject.

By this time economic liberalism, which had fought against the remnants of feudalism, found itself in a new arena. The new enemy confronting it was the protectionist policy of the government and the views of those who supported it. This confrontation is suggested by Tsuda Mamichi's article on protectionism, and by the introductory notes written by Nakamura Masanao for Hayashi Masaaki's translation of Frédéric Bastiat's *Sophismes économiques* (1845–8) as well as by the translator's own preface. Tsuda in his article states:

> Imports and exports are reciprocal. Sometimes the former may exceed the latter, but sometimes the balance swings the other way round. Just like heat and cold or ebb and flow, they fluctuate and thereby tend towards equilibrium.

In reality, too:

> For a few years after the opening of our ports exports exceeded imports, and for the next few years imports exceeded exports. For another few years to come, exports will probably be in excess. Thus imports and exports circulate according to the law of nature and never fail to bend towards equilibrium. Arts and industry grow in the meantime, so that there is nothing to fear at all.

To say that free trade caused an outflow of gold was without foundation:

> Such a theory is mistaken. Most Western political economists, with hardly any exception, agree that protective duties do not benefit but harm a nation.[11]

Probably Tsuda was not a recent convert to this view, since he had studied under Simon Vissering, the then Professor at Leiden University, who had subscribed to Bastiat's doctrine, as we shall see in more detail later.

Nakamura's criticism of protectionism was substantially the same as Tsuda's. In the preface that he wrote for Hayashi's translation he said that the outflow of gold was caused not so much by the import of foreign goods as by the much heavier government expenditure in sending students abroad, in employing foreigners, and in purchasing weapons, warships and the like. Those who argued for protective duties did not know that economic affairs, like the flow of water, are ruled only by the laws of nature.[12] This view of Nakamura's was shared by Hayashi. Referring to his motive for translating Bastiat's book, Hayashi stated that, while there were many scholars and journalists who were acquainted with the work of H. C. Carey and who consequently advocated protective duties, there were only a few who were learned enough to be acquainted with free trade theories and their truth.[13] Thus, there really were protectionists in those days, among whom the most distinguished were Wakayama Norikazu, Sugi Koji, Ushiba Takuzo and Nishimura Shigeki.

It was Wakayama who was the first to express a protectionist view. He did so in popular terms and yet in a theoretical way. As early as 1871, only three years after the Restoration, he wrote on protective duties. Free trade, he asserted, was good enough in theory but not in practice. Although it was claimed that free trade brought about the wealth and strength of a nation, it was not practical to adopt the principle in such a country as Japan where the majority of people were still poor, unfamiliar with manufacturing and commerce, and too unenlightened to understand the public interest. There was currently an urgent need 'to prohibit the export of agricultural products and thereby to recover the fertility of the soil, to prevent the activities of cunning merchants and thereby to rescue trade from decay, to prohibit the import of, or levy heavy duties on, foreign goods, and thereby to encourage useful industries', in short, to apply protectionist policy.[14] It is clear that Wakayama's standpoint was taken from Carey, because he says that 'according to Mr Carey, it is not force but wealth that brings about victory over enemies'. Six years later, to plead his cause still further, he translated *Sophisms of Free Trade and Popular Political Economy Examined* (1849) which was written by J. B. Byles in reply to Bastiat, and in the translator's introduction he tried to contradict liberal thought once again. No country, he wrote, had ever achieved wealth without excercising protective methods; look at France, Germany, Switzerland, Denmark, America or any other country. 'When a baby is born, is it not the duty of the parents to take care of it in every possible way until it grows old enough to be independent of them?'

It was exactly the same with a nation which was a late-starter in trade and industry. He said that if, as was the case, it was outdated to fight with arms in order to invade other countries, it was the age now to try to invade other markets with the fruits of trade and industry. In summary, his argument that 'it is as clear as day that an economic policy suitable to one country is not necessarily so to another', and, accordingly, that 'it is absurd to believe that there is a general rule which applies in any country'[15] was in effect the same as the core proposition stressed by the German historical school as opposed to the British classical political economists.

The arguments with which Wakayama defended his cause offered a common basis for other protectionists. Thus his view that it was absurd to take free trade as a general rule that could apply anywhere any time was shared by Sugi Koji. Foreign trade, Sugi believed, must at any rate be balanced. Regardless of what the situation might be in the future, when the country had been developed sufficiently to compete with other countries in trade, it would at least 'for some time to come . . . be the best policy to aim at the development of our trade by protective means'.[16]

Similarly, Ushiba Takuzo, in his article written for the explicit purpose of answering the liberal Tsuda, stated that, should a country short of capital, industry and commerce indulge in trade with another country well provided in these respects, the result must surely be that gold would flow out, land would fall into devastation, production would sink and wealth would decrease. He wrote:

> Even the free-trader Mr Mill once said that the recent rise in the price of land and produce in America was a result of the rapid growth in industry there. This is enough to prove the effectiveness of the protective system, since the country has been trying to protect its own industry by means of customs. . . . So this is clearly a free-trader contradicting himself.[17]

Nishimura Shigeki was as much a traditionalist and nationalist in his economic thought as he was in his moral thought, though he was far from a fanatic like Sada who condemned every shade of Westernization. His defence of protective duties was by and large the same as Wakayama's, since he wrote:

> Those who clamorously support free trade probably see Britain flourish by free trade and believe that we ought to follow suit. But there is nothing in common in the trade of the two countries. The British opened their foreign trade of their own accord, whereas we were forced to do so by America. They are smart in mind and skilled in manufacture, whereas we are

> simple-minded and untrained in manufacture. With them land is used to the full and people are industrious, whereas this is in no way the case with us. When they started free trade, they had already excelled other nations in manufacture and commerce, whereas when we opened our trade, other nations had already surpassed us. With all of these taken into consideration, it could not be more evident that we ought not to follow free trade.

Nishimura noted that Americans, for all their superiority over Japan, were inferior to Europeans, and so put heavy customs on their imports in order to protect their own industry. Furthermore, even Britain, before Adam Smith, had done the same. Therefore, he concluded, only when Japan's industry and commerce had surpassed those of other nations and its land and labour powers had been fully utilized, would it be time for the country to adopt a policy of free trade.[18]

Related to these discussions between the opposing camps, two points may be made. The first is that protectionists, just like liberals, asked for, and stood upon, the authority of the political economists of the West. During the first twenty years of the Meiji era the writings of several Western protectionists were translated into Japanese. Outstanding among these was the work of H. C. Carey, translated in 1874 and again in 1884, whose theory gave the greatest support to the Japanese protectionists. Besides him, and J. B. Byles mentioned above, J. J. Lalor and R. E. Thompson were translated in 1877 and 1878 respectively. The second point is that two economic periodicals were launched to defend the opposing views. The first was the *Tokyo Keizai Zasshi* (Tokyo Economist), started in 1879 by the liberal Taguchi Ukichi, and the second was the *Tokai Keizai Shinpo* (Tokai New Economic Review), started in the following year by the protectionist Inugai Tsuyoshi, who is better known for his later career as a politician. The latter periodical was short-lived, but the former enjoyed a fairly long life, though not as long as that of the above-mentioned periodical started by Amano a little later. Each contained numerous articles written to refute its opponent. Taguchi's assertions were much the same as those of Kanda, Tsuda and their associates, while Inugai's opinions resembled the views expressed by other protectionists. For example, he stated:

> National economy is different from 'cosmopolite economy' and so it is from 'private economy'. . . . As all nations are not alike in race, language, custom, institution, law, and civilization,

> so they cannot help differing in their interests. What is harmful or beneficial to one nation is not necessarily so to another.

Inugai's reference to economic liberalism as 'cosmopolitism' and his related affirmation that it is utterly idle talk is reminiscent of Friedrich List's words to like effect.[19]

Idle talk or not, however, liberalism was part of the policy practised by the government. Or, to be more correct, liberalism on the one hand and protectionism on the other had to be practised according to the particular need at the time. For instance, the decision made by the government in 1880–1 for the transfer of government-owned enterprise to private firms and the ordinance issued by the Ministry of Agriculture and Trade in 1881, which promoted freedom of economic activities for the people, clearly represented the liberal side of the story. Yet the disposal of government-owned properties at low prices, together with other policies such as the financial aid and other privileges given to private firms, resulted in the growth of *zaibatsu*. Thus, when Taguchi tried to justify himself some years later, saying that Japan had been making *laissez-faire* its policy, and that the policy proved to be sound by contemporary economic development,[20] he must be said to have been only partly right.

The growth of *zaibatsu*, for good or ill, promoted a capitalist economy and the promotion of capitalism was inevitably accompanied by social problems. Workers' and peasants' disputes occurred in various parts of the country. Unfortunately for the government, these coincided with political disputes by left-wing liberals which were also at their peak throughout the country. It was against such a background that a new phase of economic thinking was initiated, characterized by the introduction of the ideas of the German historical school, the establishment of the Society for Social Policy, the Japanese counterpart or copy of the *Verein für Sozialpolitik* in Germany, and the early influence of socialist and anarchist thought.

Friedrich List was for the first time translated, though only in part, in 1889, A. H. G. Wagner in 1895, W. H. Roscher in 1896, G. F. von Schönberg in 1897, and Lujo Brentano in 1889. Following the theories of List and Roscher, Oshima Sadamasu believed that when a country was in an underdeveloped state, free trade should be adopted, but if it had been developed to such an extent that its people could appreciate the benefit of foreign trade, protection must be the policy. When the country reached the state of development sufficient for it to compete with others, then free trade must again be adopted.

Therefore the liberal policy practised in the earlier part of the era was not harmful. On the contrary, it was profitable, because without it feudal elements that had survived the upheaval of the Restoration would not have been removed. 'It resembles Adam Smith standing up to stifle the mercantilist system to death.' But it was profitable only then. To speak for liberalism at this stage was absolutely wrong. 'People tend to be attracted by the word "freedom" but freedom in politics and freedom in foreign trade are entirely different from each other. The former liberates a nation, whereas the latter liberates other nations at the expense of one nation.' Liberals such as Taguchi and his friends were 'short-sighted', since the Japanese economy had developed not because of, as they wrongly supposed, but in spite of, the low customs duties. These were the burden forced upon Japan by means of the unequal treaties; a burden which the nation should attempt at any cost to cast off by way of treaty revision.[21]

About this time the modern history of Japan was marking a turning point. The German influence was growing more and more prevalent in all ways in place of that of the British or French. A long discussion over the possible constitution ended in the eventual victory of the German school. The Imperial Constitution, after the German model, was promulgated in 1889 and the first Imperial Diet was convened in the following year. Following such trends, the Imperial Rescript on Education, which was drafted on nationalist lines by the Confucian Motoda Nagazane, was also issued in 1890. Chapter 9 of this book, though not concerning economic thought as such, may throw light on such a process. Protectionists or nationalists were now seen to be on the offensive and the liberals on the defensive. This may be illustrated by Taguchi's article, apologetically entitled 'Free trade theory does not neglect the nation', in which he wrote: 'Free traders do not argue that their policy ought to be pursued because it is a truth, even if our thirty-eight million people should starve to death. On the contrary, they speak for their theory because they believe that it benefits the nation.'[22]

Agreement on the revision of the treaties between Japan and the countries concerned was reached in 1894–7 and the Sino–Japanese War ended in Japan's victory in 1895. These events gave a great impetus to industrialization, to such an extent indeed that this period was subsequently regarded by some students of Japanese history as the onset of the 'Japanese Industrial Revolution'. But regardless of whether or not it represented the onset of the Industrial Revolution, this new development inevitably gave rise, as mentioned above, to the problems peculiar to any industrial society. A factory law to regulate working hours and other labour conditions began to be discussed, though the actual enactment was delayed until towards the end of the era. Here again liberals were opposed to it because of their conviction that, left alone, everything would go right and that the shortening of working hours and similar matters were the business of the parties concerned and certainly not of the law. In contrast, a group of scholars, of whom Kanai Noburu, Kuwata Kumazo and their friends were the leading members, gathered to discuss social problems and organized the Society for Social Policy in 1896.

In the meantime the ideas of the social policy school in Germany had been introduced to Japanese readers by Wadagaki Kenzo in his article published eight years before the establishment of the Society. On the problem of poverty, he explained, there had been two distinct schools of political economists, namely the conservative or *laissez-faire* school on the one hand, and the radical or socialist school on the other. The former, to which Adam Smith, David Ricardo and their disciples belonged, proposed self-help and progress, and the latter, to which Robert Owen, J. K. Rodbertus, P. J. Proudhon, Ferdinand Lassalle, Karl Marx and the like belonged, proposed co-operation and revolution. 'Between these two, however, there is an independent school which is not satisfied either with conservatism and progress or with radicalism and revolution.' This was the social policy school.[23] Kanai had also performed the same task of introducing the same principle in his article written five years after Wadagaki's. Criticizing G. E. Boissonade's article on labour problems in Japan,[24] he wrote: 'I cannot possibly agree with him, who still clings to the illusion of natural law in jurisprudence and to the old-fashioned doctrines in political economy such as J. B. Say's and C. F. Bastiat's.' He supported only the legal protection of child labour. Why not take further steps to accept 'the new doctrine of social policy'? The Factory Act of Britain had evidently proved that the theory of *laissez-faire*, which prevailed so much in Britain itself, was no more than a day-dream.[25]

Such was the basic idea held in common by those who gathered to organize the Society, as indeed was made clear in the 'Programme of the Society for Social Policy' which was published four years later:

> It is a great pleasure for us to see that recently the trade and industry of this country have made great progress and the wealth

> of this nation has attained remarkable growth. However, there are symptoms of an increase in the inequality between the rich and the poor and of the disruption of social harmony. In particular, disputes between capital and labour are already making their appearance. It is impossible not to be upset at the thought of it. We fear that unless something is done to remedy the situation, it will be too late tomorrow. . . . We object to *laissez-faire*, because excessive self-interest and unlimited free competition can only add to the aforementioned inequality. We also object to socialism, because an attempt to overthrow the existing economic system and to exterminate the capitalist class can only harm the development of the nation. Our aim is to maintain the present economic order based on private ownership and, within that boundary, to prevent class antagonism and to achieve social harmony through the activities of individuals on the one hand and the power of the state on the other.[26]

Naturally enough, the Society had to fight on two fronts. Taguchi, the leader of his camp, wrote in defence of his cause that labour conditions should be settled by both parties concerned and not by a factory law. If a labourer was dissatisfied with his work, he had only to quit it for a new job. If conditions were unreasonable, workers could unite to oppose them. 'Who decided that to work more than eight hours is bad for health?' There was nothing to justify state intervention in private matters.[27] This assertion was denied by Toyohara Matao, who commented that 'the argument of the political economists who support individualism is wrong not only in the premise but also in the conclusion'. Their premise was that people are independent of one another, but this was untenable. Their conclusion was that, being independent, people should be left absolutely free unless they impeded the freedom of others, but this, according to Toyohara, was not tenable either:

> People are social beings unable to live by themselves. Society and the state, therefore, are indispensable conditions for their existence and development. Should the freedom of each individual ever be allowed to expand to such an extent as to make society and the state unsustainable, then, even though that expansion might not be impeding the freedom of others, the very condition of human existence and development must necessarily be annihilated.

According to the individualists, the only matters to be left to the state were military and judicial affairs. And yet such was the current poverty of the workers that the majority of people were afraid of the possible result. 'This is why I object to the political economists who propound individualism, and why I insist that it is the duty of the state to remedy the misery of the workers.'

To Toyohara socialism was just as untenable. 'Socialists are mistaken', he proclaimed, 'in their supposition that all persons are equal.' On the contrary, he argued, they were by nature different in physical strength, mental faculty and in all other points. Every inequality in the existing system of society arose from these differences. This being so, even a powerful attempt to remove the inequality once and far all would be only temporarily successful, if at all. Socialists wanted and believed it possible, to abolish private ownership and to let everyone work in publicly owned industries, but this would be fruitless, leading only to total disaster:

> The difficulty of nationalizing so great a variety of industries run by so large a number of individuals is beyond all imagination. Besides, even if nationalization were possible, to allot each different type of work to each different individual according to the person's best aptitude would be simply impossible and to distribute the fruits of work in any impartial way would be even more difficult.

Socialists were mistaken in other respects too. For instance:

> Those who support socialism have recourse to the Smithian and Ricardian doctrine that labour is not only the cause but also the standard of the price of a commodity, and they develop it even further to say that labour is the cause of production and property the effect of labour, and that capitalists are therefore the usurpers of that which should belong to labourers. To show the error of this argument is easy enough because . . . though labour may influence the price of commodity, the influence of supply and demand is by far the greater. In other words, labour is neither the only cause of price nor the standard of it. Labour, along with natural power and capital, is only one of the elements of production.

When all of this was taken into account, socialism became unacceptable. The misery of workers should be remedied by state intervention and not by radical destruction of the present order of society.[28]

Kuwata also attacked socialism in his book *Oshu Rodo Mondai no Taisei* (Outline of Labour Problems in Europe, 1899), two chapters of which he devoted to an examination of the 'Errors of Socialism' and the 'Necessity of Social Reform'. He believed that a socialist state was merely a chimera that could exist only in the mind of those such as Abe Iso. No person would have freedom of choice in wages or in employment, because such matters would be managed by the state. And yet the state could not have any proper standard by which to decide what work would be suitable for each individual or what wages would be reasonable for every type of employment. Consequently, the result would only be a system of forced labour. 'How different would people be from slaves? Who would wish to live in such a society?' Socialism based on materialism was also wrong. Karl Marx's interpretation was that the growth of productive power leads by the increased application of machinery to a decrease in the demand for labour, and consequently an increase in the number of the poor. But this was true only in the short run. 'The statistics on the poor in Britain in the latter half of the nineteenth century shows that, contrary to Marx's assumption, the number of the poor has steadily decreased.' The introduction of new machinery in the spinning industry, for instance, might cause a decrease in the demand for labour in the mills, but might also bring about an increase in labour demand in the machine industry, which, in its turn, might give rise to the need for more hands in the iron industry, then in the coal-mining industry, and so on. In short, it must be said that 'the application of machinery both decreases and increases the demand for labour'.[29]

The tone of Kuwata's words so far may sound as if they were those of an advocate of *laissez-faire*. But, in fact, the conclusion arising from all of his critical comments was that socialism is so groundless that 'it cannot be of any help in the solution of labour problems'.[30]

The real solution as he saw it was social policy. No further comments are necessary here, because what he said about social policy is roughly the same as the arguments of Toyohara or Kanai. In any case, since the standpoint of the social policy school was so middle-of-the-road, it was vulnerable to attack or counter-attack from the two opposing camps. Besides the criticism by the liberal school already described, an attack was launched from the socialist side as well. Kuwata's accusation was immediately answered by the socialist Unitarian Abe,[31] but the speeches, or rather the debates, made at a meeting held in 1899 in preparation for organizing a printers' union are perhaps even more interesting. Kanai, Kuwata and

Katayama Sen, who was later to become a well-known communist but at that time was a social democrat, were there as speakers. Kuwata spoke against socialism and for social harmony, that is to say, the harmony between capital and labour. To this Katayama replied:

> Harmony between capital and labour may indeed be necessary. But in the present circumstances there can never be any kind of harmony between them. To talk about it at present is most impractical. All that exists now is the relationship between lord and vassal. No, it is more than that; it is the relationship between master and slave. . . . To realize true harmony, we ought to let the workers hoist their flag. . . . That is why trade unions are necessary and why their strikes must also be necessary.[32]

For him the aim of the labour movement had to be:

> To make workers unite in trade unions or to let them organize economic associations such as co-operative shops and factories and to let those unions participate in political movements, and, with the power thus acquired, to realize socialism, the final goal of the workers.[33]

Against this, Kanai, speaking after Katayama, denounced socialism and advised the workers present to be concerned only with economic purposes. Here we see that the contrasting attitudes towards labour problems between socialism and co-operation of capital and labour had thus already become apparent.

Meanwhile, Abe, Katayama and others, with Kotoku Denjiro (Shusui), who was later to become an infamous anarchist and to be sentenced to death, had organized the Society for the Study of Socialism in 1898. The next year it was reorganized as the Socialist Society and again as the Social Democratic Party. The Party published a 'Declaration' stating that the parliament as it stood should really be called 'a congress of the rich' and calling for the public ownership of all land and capital, the equal distribution of property, and certain other items of a more political kind such as universal suffrage and the abolition of the death penalty.[34] Such a declaration doubtless seemed too provocative and certainly too dangerous to the establishment. The immediate dissolution of the Party was ordered and the newspapers in which the 'Declaration' was printed were also immediately stopped.

The Society for Social Policy then published a statement, apparently in order to prevent its principles from being confused with socialism by the authorities, or its being regarded by them as a 'dangerous thought'. After repeating the Society's objection to socialism and *laissez-faire*, the statement read:

> There have recently appeared in this country some people who openly advocate socialism, and there are some who tend to neglect the difference between social policy and socialism and confound our principle with socialism. Social policy is compatible with the peace and order of the country, whereas socialism cannot be realized without overthrowing the existing order of the state and society. This is accepted by every science of society and even socialists agree with it.[35]

To the critics this must have seemed to be a ridiculously cowardly attitude. Naturally, to such an economic liberal as Taguchi, there seemed to be little difference between both principles, at least in their aims, since both called for a factory law, the protection of workers, restriction of working hours and the like. To a socialist such as Abe, social policy appeared to be only a step towards socialism and consequently the difference between them seemed to be only a matter of degree. Without denying the difference between the two principles, Kawakami Hajime, who was later to be a celebrated Marxist but at that time was merely a humanitarian thinker, said that the statement was no more than an apology, designed to defend themselves at the expense of others.[36]

Socialism as a thought, if not as a political organization, continued to survive in spite of such suppressive policies as the Preservation of the Peace Act[37] and the Newspaper Act in 1900 and 1909 respectively. A number of socialist books were written by Abe, Katayama, Kotoku and others. Some works by Marx and Engels and others by the anarchist Kropotkin were made available in translation to the workers and intellectuals of the day. Yet for the time being the social policy school still obtained. In 1907 when the Society assumed every appearance of an academic society and decided to hold a general meeting and to publish its own bulletin regularly, its members included prominent intellectuals and professors of the time, with Fukuda Tokuzo, the most brilliant of all, among them. As the number of its members grew, so did its fame, so much so indeed that it was sometimes called the 'parliament of professors'.[38] Thus, although there is reason to believe that during the era under consideration Japan may have embarked on the path leading towards the severe repression not only of socialist thought but also of the ideas of social policy, this was a development which did not, in fact, occur until a later period, a period which may fittingly be called the Dark Ages of modern Japan.

2

THE ECONOMIC THOUGHT OF NISHI AMANE

The first pages of the first issue of the journal *Meiroku Zasshi* were allotted to an article by Nishi Amane. The journal was published by a society by the name of Meirokusha (Meiji Six Society) which comprised some learned people who were concerned about the enlightenment of their compatriots. As though representing the concern and zeal of his colleagues, Nishi wrote:

> In our talk among friends we often tend to make comparisons with European countries, when we envy them and lament how unenlightened we are. Eventually, after concluding that nothing can be done about the ignorance of our people, we can only heave a deep sigh. Since the Restoration plenty men of ability have emerged, many laws and regulations have been reformed and, from the government at the top down to many prefectures, all things have ceased to be what they were in the old days. There have indeed been countless good policies and fine plans and yet they have not successfully reached the people at large. The reason is that it has not been long enough since the Restoration to achieve inward renewal, in spite of the outward show of progress.[1]

What Nishi proposed as the best way to carry out the urgent task of enlightenment was to establish and popularize the means of writing all Japanese words in European letters. After enumerating the possible merits and demerits that might accompany the proposal, he concluded that the former would never fail to surpass the latter. As such an argument might suggest, he was more philosophically than economically or politically minded.

Although Nishi, as well as Tsuda and Fukuzawa, were distinguished thinkers in the days of the Japanese Enlightenment, the first two, unlike Fukuzawa, left behind no systematic body of economic writing. Yet, like many writers in the age of Enlightenment in the West, they were concerned with most aspects of human interest, and so with economic matters as well. The economic thought of Nishi and Tsuda, which is exemplified in some of their articles, lecture notes and manuscripts, was undoubtedly liberal, formed most probably under the influence of Simon Vissering at Leiden, under whom both of them studied, as referred to in the previous chapter.

Although Vissering was then professor of political economy at the University of Leiden, he had practised law after graduating from Leiden and before going back there as an assistant to Professor Thorbecke, who was later to become prime minister. This was by no means an exceptional case in the Continental countries. Thus it was quite natural that Vissering lectured to his two private students from Japan in as many as 'five subjects', composed of legal as well as economic disciplines.

Like other thinkers in the Japanese Enlightenment, Nishi started his career as a thinker by denouncing the moral philosophy of Confucianism which had prevailed for so long in feudal Japan. In a manuscript entitled 'Shohaku Sakki' (1863) he wrote that 'it is much too loose a doctrine for Confucians to teach that everything ranging from natural phenomena, such as wind and rain, to all human affairs is regulated by one and the same everlasting and invariable law of nature.' Such a theory gave rise to a groundless belief, based on sheer delusion, that 'an eclipse of the sun or of the moon, a bad harvest, floods, etc. are all attributed to the policy of the government or of the emperor'.[2]

'Physical law', as Nishi put it, 'is a law of nature which, like gravitation, is a necessity which must be obeyed regardless of any human will.' The Mongolian invasion of Japan in the thirteenth century failed not as a result, as had so far been believed, of the prayers of some Buddhist priests such as Nichiren but because of the typhoon which occurred in so timely a fashion and which ruined the entire Mongolian fleet.[3]

Physical law and moral law are thus different from each other. 'Moral law is *a posteriori* but is far from being wilful or contrived. It is a law all the same.' The unchanging nature of the law lies in the human propensity for love and hate, common to every human being, whether Eastern or Western, and that propensity for love and hate is based on pleasure and pain. This Benthamite philosophy is the essence of Nishi's *Hyakuichi Shinron* (Uniformity of All Learnings Reviewed), 1874.[4] Thus Nishi's human law, represented by love and hate like Bentham's pleasure and pain, leads to the world of morals and legislation and not directly to that of economy, as Smithian self-interest or one's desire to improve one's conditions does. And yet it is true that it indirectly opens the way to the latter.

In that sense a series of articles entitled 'Jinsei Sanbosetsu' (Three Treasures of Life) is also worthy of note. It was written soon after the aforementioned book, under the clear influence of J. S. Mill's *Utilitarianism* (1863) which Nishi admired as enlarging and yet greatly modifying Bentham's theory. The ultimate state of well-being, or general welfare, was made the 'first and foremost aim of human life', and the means for realizing this state were 'first, health; second, knowledge; and third, wealth', which together constitute the 'three treasures of life'.[5] They are the essential basis of society and manifest the distinction between civilized and savage states. In the savage state they are hardly esteemed, whereas in the civilized state they are esteemed greatly.

The first characteristic of his argument here is that people are deemed equal in the desire for those treasures so that everybody ought to be left free in their conduct unless it debases them. Nishi called this principle of equality and freedom a Western or Christian one, saying that 'it has not been known to us in the East until now but without it the morality of the three treasures can never stand'. The hereditary rank systems prevailing under despotism or feudalism, to say nothing of the caste system in India, are most inconsistent with the three-treasure morality.[6] The second characteristic is that Nishi reduced the treasures to private interest: 'If it did not benefit oneself, who would strive for the sake of others?' This is only too evident from everyone's own experience. While it is true that the aim of society is the 'public interest', called 'general welfare', without private interest there can be no public interest, which is nothing but the 'aggregate of the former', and private interest consists in sound body, developed knowledge and increased wealth, that is to say, three treasures. So if one should wish to attain morality, one must start from respecting one's own three treasures.[7]

All of these discussions are moral and have little to do with economic matters. However, if the pursuit of those 'three treasures' must be left free, then the pursuit of material well-being, i.e. wealth, as one of the three, should also be free – a conviction which necessarily leads to economic liberalism. In the economic part of his private lectures, 'Hyakugaku Renkan' (All Learnings Combined), Nishi distinguishes between economy and political economy, saying that economy is a way by which a private person can attain wealth, whereas political economy is a science whereby a nation can attain wealth.[8] Starting with this definition, he then traces the history of political economy from Giovanni Botero to J. S. Mill via Quesnay, Gournay, Turgot, Hume, Steuart, Smith, Malthus, Say, Ricardo and James Mill, referring also to Sismondi, Whateley, Senior and Vissering. He divided his lectures into a number of parts, i.e. society, production (and the division of labour), product, value, price, exchange, money and circulation, capital and stock, interest and profit, credit, paper money or banknotes, the principles of taxation, and consumption, thus proving that he had a fairly systematic plan of political economy in mind, resembling by and large that of J. S. Mill. The resemblance goes even further because he says, as though copying Mill, that 'production follows natural law but distribution human law'. Like Mill, who proceeded from there to the description and systematic examination of socialist thought as propounded by Owen, Saint-Simon and Fourier, Nishi also refers to those names, though, unlike Mill, only to denounce their thought. While enumerating as untenable, from what he regards as the political economy point of view, a number of items such as monopoly, guilds and protectionism, he adds to these some more items just as untenable: socialism, communism and Fourierism.[9] This divergence from Mill's way of thought must have come from the influence of economic thought then prevailing in Holland, where he had studied.[10] But, even more basically, the divergence must result from the difference between Mill's Britain, where the Industrial Revolution was nearly complete and where social problems inherent in the developed state of capitalist society were apparent, and Nishi's Japan where the industrialized state still belonged to a distant future. Or, it may also be that Nishi believed in economic liberalism to such an extent as to identify the socialist criticism of private ownership with the intervention in it by the state. He thus subscribed to the system of *laissez-faire* by rejecting mercantilist and other restrictive systems on the one hand, and socialism on the other as another sort of state intervention in private property. Apart from socialism, he enumerates 'some items which cannot apply in political economy': 'first monopoly, second guilds, third protectionism, fourth restrictive and prohibiting systems, fifth mercantilist systems, sixth usury law, seventh repression of luxury, and eighth government interference'. Regarding the fifth item, he says that Spain cannot thrive because it has prohibited the importation of foreign goods, seeking to acquire gold and silver only by the export of its own produce. Or, with regard to the sixth item, he says that since capital is the result of labour, and labour has to be rewarded, and the reward depends on objective circumstances, interest rates should be free from government intervention. But he puts the greatest stress on the third item, saying that 'three kinds of protection, i.e. protective duties in agriculture, manufacture and commerce, are what stand accused most in political economy'. Nishi inserts an English sentence into his Japanese text: 'When they [individuals] prosecute the branches of industry advantageous to themselves, they are necessarily also prosecuting such as are advantageous to [the] public.'[11]

In an article which he contributed to *Meiroku Zasshi* (Meiji Six Journal) on the question of whether foreigners should be allowed to travel freely inside Japan, he proves that his attitudes are just as consistent. Like a philosopher, he argues that just as only chemical analysis can reveal if a strange fruit is or is not edible, so only logical reasoning can judge whether foreigners' free travel inside the country, which has not yet been realized, is desirable or not. Logical analysis is composed of two kinds: deductive and inductive. The former is the method by which to know that a small curve, if extended, could not fail to make a circle. To apply this method to the problem concerned, it would follow that as the opposite of a curved line is a straight line, so the opposite of open ports and friendly intercourse is closed ports and an exclusionist policy. If freedom of travel is part of the former, and if Japan has discarded the latter policy, then the answer to the problem must be clear enough. The policy of freedom of travel ought by all means to be adopted.[12] To prohibit foreigners from travelling freely after adopting the policy of friendship and open ports would be the same as heading for the Bering Sea after deciding that Australia was to be the destination.

However, for such a practical problem as this, the inductive method might be more pursuasive. As it is not possible to compare all of the merits and demerits of the matter, it might be better to leave aside positive points and to enumerate negative points in order to consider whether they might be prevented or even turned to positive effect.[13] Nishi thus enumerates some of the possible causes for complaint: that foreigners might trade not only in the open ports but also elsewhere, or that they might step into prohibited districts, or that the interpreters might sometimes be embarrassed at being unable to understand foreigners, or that foreigners might be accompanied by dogs. He claims that all of these can be prevented beforehand by the stipulation of necessary conditions, and that there will consequently be nothing negative and that everything will become positive.[14] Like a true devotee of enlightenment, Nishi discusses much in this way, which may again serve to show his philosophical leanings. However, such recourse to logical terms was in fact no more than a device, his real intention here being to propose *laissez-faire* in one of the issues of the day. This view was also shared by Tsuda, though his approach was quite different, and more practical (see Chapter 3). Thus, the characteristic feature of Nishi's argument may be made clearer by comparison with an opposing opinion on the matter, which was held by Fukuzawa.

Fukuzawa intentionally mimics Nishi's logic in order to contradict the latter, as we shall see later. It is indeed true, he admits, that induction is the method by which to know the whole from its part. Just as Nishi says, one could easily presume the shape of a cup, i.e. a circle, from a little piece of it, i.e. an arch. A small shift in the position of a star would suggest its orbit. However, the same method can also be used to reach the opposite conclusion: 'Should the international situation since the opening of our ports be regarded as a loss to our side, it could lead us to consider that the whole might be a great loss in the end. The recent increase in foreign loans, for example, is like a little shift of a star from which to guess its whole orbit.' Then, why 'a loss to our side'? The reason is simply that 'the difference in faculties between foreigners and Japanese is such that the trade between both can only cause a loss to us'. Nishi says that the period of seven years that has passed since the Restoration has brought about a complete change in the nation. But it is not true. What has changed is only the government and not the people at large. So, when one talks about anything that concerns a national interest such as foreigners' free travel in Japan, one ought to start from the premise that 'the effect of the Restoration has not yet reached the lowest level of the people's consciousness'. The same thing also applies to induction. Nishi enumerates a number of possible mischiefs caused by freedom but the policy that he recommends seems far from effective. 'Can a mere stipulation be of any effect in the present state of things?' The point is that we are not standing on an equal footing with foreigners. To permit freedom of travel to foreigners will necessarily lead to allowing them to reside freely among the Japanese, which again will naturally lead to free trade, and free trade is a one-sided benefit to the more advanced, i.e. foreigners.[15]

Thus, the confrontation between Fukuzawa and Nishi about the problem of foreigners' freedom of travel originated in their different views on the rights and wrongs of free trade. Just as Fukuzawa was against it, so was Nishi for it. Common to both of them, however, was the consideration of which would benefit the nation more. National interest, in the sense of what would best serve the enlightenment and modernization of the nation, ought to have priority.

About the same time, Nishi wrote another unpublished manuscript entitled 'Shakaitoron no Setsu' (On Socialism). Socialism, along with nihilism, is nothing but a variation of the ancient communism proposed by Plato. Nishi thus contrasts communism with political economy. Though there have been scholars in every age who uphold communism, it has never been realized. On the other hand, political economy has become more and more popular in the past two or three hundred years. Communism aims at equality, whereas political economy admits inequality. Communism restricts industriousness as a cause of inequality in wealth and represses luxury as a result of industriousness, whereas political economy leaves both labour and consumption to everyone's free choice. If the political economy of modern times is incompatible with the communism of ancient times, it is equally so with the latter's modern revival, namely socialism and nihilism. These aim to overturn existing society, whereas political economy regards it as a natural outcome of human nature.[16]

Here again we see that Nishi finds the basic character of political economy in private ownership and freedom. Nishi concludes:

> Those who are in charge of the government should keep all of these matters under consideration. As in Germany and Russia, when socialist and other sects have become too strong, it would be hard to check them. The best policy is to prevent them beforehand.

He does not say anything about what to do in order to 'prevent them beforehand' or about what that best policy has to do with political economy, and yet this article, though not published, is, along with 'Hyakugaku Renkan', one of the earliest attempts at explaining what socialist theories are and one of the very first proposals made in Japan for the consideration of possible counter-measures. The basic standpoint of the article is that of economic liberalism, and is thus completely in agreement with the assumption made in 'Hyakugku Renkan' that socialism is the most detested by and the least acceptable to political economy.

3

THE ECONOMIC THOUGHT OF TSUDA MAMICHI

Among the writers at the time of the Meiji Enlightenment, Tsuda Mamichi may well be said to be among those who best personified the spirit of enlightenment. Even in commonplace matters he tried to promulgate a rational way of thinking, as is the case with, for example, his articles 'Fukushoron' (On Official Insignia), 'Tengu-setsu' (On Long-nosed Goblins), 'Kaisetsu' (On Ghosts) or 'Fufu Dokenben' (On the Equal Rights of Husband and Wife).

In the essay 'Fukushoron' he argues that, apart from the military officers whose duty it is to subdue violence by means of violence, civil servants have no need of insignia or uniforms varying from rank to rank: 'Nowadays civil servants in European and American countries all wear the same formal clothes, from the emperor or king or president down to the commoner.' The reason for this is that, unlike military government, civil government is government by means of morals and laws and so has no need of rank or robe. When Tsuda saw the Dutch consul in Hong Kong, when he was on his way back from Holland where he had been studying, he was surprised to find the consul dressed in an ostentatious uniform. When Tsuda asked why, the consul smiled and replied that that was the only way to convince the Asian savage of the greatness of the Dutch consul.[1] Writing in this way, Tsuda no doubt implies that the Japanese, too, are among those 'Asian savages' who must by all means be enlightened.

Referring in the above-mentioned articles to legendary beings such as long-nosed goblins and the like, Tsuda states that only the Japanese are so unenlightened as to believe in these mythical creatures, and that those who have reached a certain stage of civilization are free from all such nonsensical beliefs. Here again we see that the civilization of Europe is contrasted with the uncivilized state of Asians, or Japanese.[2]

Something quite similar is seen in his article 'Fufu Dokenben'.

Distinguishing the equality between men and women from that between husband and wife, he denies the latter but approves of the former, again referring to the civil laws in European and American countries where, he says, there are no distinctions made between men and women in both personal and real rights.[3]

Tsuda, who thus regarded the belief in goblins and the like as sheer irrationality to be overcome by civilization, later goes so far as to claim himself to be a materialist. In other words, for him the hallmark of value lies in Western civilization in general and in materialistic rationalism in particular. He says: 'In Europe spiritualism and materialism have long existed, never ceasing to contradict each other, and it is the latter that I support', because 'spiritualism is no more than an unfounded illusion like a mirage'.[4] As for science and learning, he divides them into the 'real' and the 'vain'. By vain learning he implies the traditional theories based on Confucianism or varieties of its sects that had prevailed for so long, and by real learning he means 'Western astronomy, physics, chemistry, medicine, political economy, and Greek philosophy, all of which are based on ascertained realities'. To Tsuda, civilization seemed to be simply the state of affairs in which 'real studies prevail and everyone is well acquainted with reason'. However, even Europe took a long time to become mature enough to reach that stage, so that it would not be easy for 'south-eastern countries' to reach it. Needless to say, once again Japan is, if only implicitly, counted among those 'south-eastern countries'. There religion, as well as or even more than science, contributes to the general education of the people at large. There are varieties of religion such as Shintoism and Buddhism in Japan, with Christianity, Islam, etc. in foreign countries. Of these, Tsuda claims, Christianity in general and Protestantism in particular are the best, since the latter is the richest in freedom and therefore the nearest to civilization. Thus, he proposed to employ overseas Protestant missionaries in the same way as foreigners employed for teaching science and technology.[5]

It might seem strange for Tsuda to propose the promotion of a religious belief; he who claims to prefer 'materialism' to 'spiritualism', and 'real' learning to 'vain' learning. For him, however, religion is no more than a means. In other words, just as it takes time 'to achieve a civilized state by real learning prevailing among the general mass of people', for the time being recourse must be had to religion, especially to its most liberal variety.[6] It was in a way consistent for Tsuda to judge religion according to the degree of liberty of which it approved.

Yet such an argument had naturally to be contradicted from the standpoint of freedom of conscience. For example, Nishi Amane criticized him in an article 'Kyomonron' (On Religious Sects)[7] and Mori Arinori in 'Kyoshu' (On Religious Belief).[8]

Thus, for Tsuda, enlightenment and freedom were inseparable. When discussing the freedom of the press, he says that the difference between the civilized and uncivilized is the difference between the existence and non-existence of political restraint upon the people. 'Whether a nation is civilized or not depends on whether it enjoys freedom of speech and conduct.' Apart from the 'shameful politics of a barbarous government', suppressing its people by means of direct force, the government of a despotic or half-civilized country is apt to control its people by laws and decrees. In Britain and America people enjoy complete freedom in what they do and say, unless they interfere with the freedom of others, whereas in other countries, such as France, there are regulations which forbid the publication of printed matter without the permission of the government. Successive attempts at overthrowing the government had brought about such suppression, but this had proved to be a failure after all, as was the case at the time of Napoleon III. It is clear that the suppression of freedom resulted not in political stability but in instability. In Japan, therefore, the absolute freedom of the press should be proclaimed as soon as possible in order to help the people to become much more enlightened.[9]

Government intervention should thus be done away with in all possible ways.

> Now is the time for the culture and civilization of the Japanese Empire to start growing. When a tree is about to grow and stretch its branches, it should be given protection so that it may be kept away from interference from outside. In the same way, when people are about to develop their knowlege and culture, things ought to be left entirely to their natural course.[10]

It is obvious that the protection mentioned here has nothing to do with so-called protectionism. But it is also true that, for Tsuda, freedom and enlightenment were not so much values to be pursued for their own sake as an indispensable means to achieve wealth and strength for Japan as a modern nation. And this was also the case, as has already been expounded, with Nishi and other promoters of the Japanese Enlightenment.

The flourishing of newspapers, Tsuda writes, 'nourishes, by contributing to the progress of civilization, the very root of the wealth and strength of the country'. The combination of enlightenment and nationalism is, more often than not, a characterisic trait of intellectuals in late-starting countries, and Tsuda and his friends may be regarded as typical examples. In the enlightenment movement in the advanced countries, barbarism or an uncivilized state signified the past stage in which they had once been and civilization the present stage, whereas in the underdeveloped countries their present state represented nothing but the savage stage and civilization belonged to the future stage that was to be attained at any cost. 'National prestige' through modernization was all that could matter there.

Tsuda's argument on torture, a practice which he endeavoured to deal with severely, comes to the same conclusion. He says that 'there is no evil more lamentable than torture', but at the same time he combines this argument with the revision of the treaties. The reason why the treaties between Western countries and Japan were not on equal terms, he explains, was simply that their respective penal laws differed so much. In the West no crime was punished without evidence and, moreover, there was a system of appeal to a higher court, whereas in Japan crimes were punished on confession only and there was no system of appeal. In the Western legal system, even if there was sufficient evidence, no crime was punished unless it was explicitly stated as a crime in law, whereas in Japan it was not necessary to have a relevant legal code for a crime to be punished. Thus, it was not unreasonable that Western countries did not want their citizens living in Japan to be placed under Japanese laws. Therefore, 'if we want to make foreign residents in Japan keep our laws, we must abolish torture, and if we want to abolish torture, we must revise our penal laws'. Undoubtedly, torture was regarded as an abuse in itself but it was also an abuse that was to be abolished in order to let Japan 'stand on an equal footing with European and American countries'.[11] For Tsuda enlightenment was a means to achieve the modernization of Japan so that it could cope with advanced countries.

His argument on the problem of foreigners' free travel in the country is in the same mould.[12] As has been suggested, Tsuda argued in a different manner from Nishi, who supported freedom, and from Fukuzawa, who was opposed to it. For Tsuda, it was not as easy as it might have seemed for Japan to obtain 'two kinds of right', i.e. the right to try foreigners and the right to tax foreign goods, by the revision of the treaties. The reason for the Japanese government's unwillingness to permit foreigners to travel freely anywhere in the country was that it feared that, in the current unenlightened conditions of the nation, there might be some Japanese who, on the one hand, might commit violence against them and, on the other, might be cheated by them. Such lack of knowledge or such backwardness in enlightenment on the part of the Japanese should properly be removed by education, but the effects of school education 'cannot be realized within a short space of time'. The enlightened state of Europeans and Americans had come from the accumulated experience that they had had through world-wide trade and commerce. The best way, therefore, was to let Japanese people in general travel abroad widely and thereby accumulate experience. However, this was simply vain talk. Consequently it had to be regarded as a good opportunity for the Japanese nation to acquire experience when foreigners residing there wanted to travel inland freely. 'It is lucky for us that foreigners want to travel inside our country. They ought to be admitted at once so that they might contribute, by their communication and contact with our people, to the progress of the people's knowledge and enlightenment.'

This was clear, Tsuda assumes, from the experience of the Japanese nation at the time of opening some ports to foreign countries just over ten years previously. At that time many were of the opinion that it was the greatest calamity that had ever befallen the Japanese, but 'now it goes without saying which of the two policies, opening or closing the country to the outer world, has proved to be more beneficial'. The difference between the current state of 'enlightenment and civilization' and the circumstances preceding it is obvious and was effected in such a small space of time.

> In those days those who were aware of the superiority of the Western countries in science and arts were so few that they numbered less than twenty in medical and military professions. Those who knew anything of the legal systems, civilization and culture, or liberty and equality were next to none. Now, after so short a while, is it not amazing progress to see that even youngsters are only too ready to talk about civilization and enlightenment?

If the progress which the opening of the country had made possible in such a short while was of such a kind, then the same must also apply to foreigners' free travel in Japan. To claim that this ought not to be permitted before the right to tax and try foreigners had been secured was an argument standing on its head, because the real independence of the country could be achieved only by realizing the enlightenment of 'our people in general and those in the middling and lower stations of life in particular', for whom the freedom of foreigners to travel and thereby to associate with the people was most beneficial. Thus his ideas with regard to the enlightenment of people in the middle and lower ranks are very clear. At the same time it is worth noting that he made the realization of an 'independent free empire' the supreme aim to be achieved at any cost, for which enlightenment was believed to be a means, while at the same time he preferred the leaving of 'all affairs to their natural course', to the 'protecting of the people by the government'.

Thus he made the most of all possible opportunities to advocate freedom. His article 'Jinzairon' (People of Talent) is another example. According to Tsuda, in ancient times Asia was rich in ability, whereas in modern times Europe and America were endowed with it. Within Japan, too, regions which produced persons of distinguished talent varied from age to age, the reason for which was not very clear but might well relate to the degree of freedom. 'In Asian countries despotic monarchical governments have been prevalent which are not favourable to the development of talent, whereas in European and American countries most governments favour people's freedom, which again contributes to the growth of talent.'[13]

Arguments to a similar effect are also found in his article 'Seiron' (On Government): 'Our people have long been subject to and accustomed to an oppressive system, with the result that their human nature has been too frustrated to develop itself.' Therefore it was essential that 'the government be correct in its policy and refrain from impeding the natural progress of enlightenment', to which end it was recommended that people should be made to participate in national affairs through parliamentary elections. 'Such unrestrained human nature is the source of national vigour, and where national vigour shrinks, national prestige cannot be expected to rise.' Here, too, we see that national prestige is directly combined with 'unrestrained human nature'.

In any case, 'everything in the universe, be it physical or moral, is under the control of a rule free from human will', like a ball thrown up in the air which cannot help falling down. Although he does not explicitly use the phrase 'natural law', the phrase which was so popular in the age of Enlightenment in the West, his implicit belief in it seems evident because he says: 'Although civil laws are man-made institutions, they must be subject to the necessary regulation of nature' and 'any deviation from the latter cannot fail to cause mischievous results'. If any deviation from order results only in mischief, wilful intervention on the part of government in the matter of the education and speech of the people must also be harmful.

> To enact educational laws and to appoint teachers is harmful to the freedom of education. To have a torture system in jurisprudence is harmful to the freedom of the people. To have decrees to control the press is harmful to the freedom of publication.

Tsuda goes further than that. He claims that to widen municipal roads or to separate pedestrian and carriage ways from each other at government expense, in order to obtain a beautiful view or to ensure safety against fire and accident, is harmful because it is not the result of natural development. Referring to the contrast between Paris and London he says:

> To the south of Kyobashi, Tokyo, buildings made of bricks and stones have appeared and roads have become so wide that pedestrians and wagon traffic are completely separate; indeed the roads are as wide as the main streets in Paris, but they are made by the government and not by the people. How can it be justified to spend huge sums of money, which are levied on the people living outside Tokyo, in order to prosecute these extravagant works for the benefit of one particular part of the nation? . . . Beauty of outlook and protection from fire are all very well, but there is no justification unless they are the outcome of the natural course of developments. They are thus against the principle of equity.

The French, for their love of beauty, exploited their people to beautify Paris, and their government had often suffered popular revolts. The British, by contrast, were 'steady' and faithful to the basic principles, so that their capital, London, though not as beautiful, had long been free from civil war and popular turmoil, and 'they are, in their wealth, second to none in the whole world'.[14]

Tsuda's arguments on economic matters are very much the same in nature as those on political and legal matters, being postulated on natural freedom. He did not publish books on political economy, and he was even less inclined than Nishi systematically to express his own economic thought. Unlike Fukuzawa, neither Tsuda nor Nishi left specific writings on economic subjects but the liberal character of Tsuda's economic thought is clear enough in his piecemeal writings.

For him economic freedom was also a means to achieve 'national prestige', in the sense of the modernization of the country. It is especially evident in his article 'Unsoron' (On Transportation). In order to realize 'national prestige', it was as essential to develop transportation as it was to improve military systems and to expand education. 'To change military systems is to strengthen forces, to establish schools is to cultivate knowledge, and, in like manner, to develop transportation is to enrich a country.' But why transportation? Different countries produce different commodities, so that 'the wealth of the world can be commanded by collecting, and making use of, as many of those commodities as possible'. Therefore, the richest country is the country whose transportation is most developed. What, then, is necessary for the development of transportation? He answers:

> It is generally assumed that no other place is as rich as London, as though there were no wealth in other parts of the world. Why is it that Britain has attained such wealth? It is simply because Britain enjoys the benefit of transportation more than any other country. The convenience of transportation in Britain indeed results from its favourable geographical position compared with any other country, but it also results from its people, who compete with each other both in intellect and in labour. . . . How is it that they can expand their knowledge and strive so hard? It is mainly on account of their government's securing for their people unrestricted freedom.

Thus he asserts that, in order to develop transportation and thereby to realize national wealth, it is essential for 'the people to be provided with the unrestrained right to freedom', and that the best example of this is to be found in Britain.[15]

The liberal character of Tsuda's economic thought is even more apparent in his articles 'Hogozei o Hitosuru Setsu' (Protective Duties criticized) and 'Boeki Kenkoron' (On the Balance of Trade).[16] With these Tsuda anticipated the full-scale controversy for and against protection which arose later between Taguchi Ukichi in his *Tokyo Keizai Zasshi* (Tokyo Economist) and Inugai Tsuyoshi in his *Tokai Keizai Shinpo* (Tokai New Economic Review), as we shall see later. In 'Hogozei o Hitosuru Setsu' Tsuda states that, according to those who advocated protection, imports had exceeded exports in recent years and that, together with the enormous salaries paid to foreign employees and the interest paid on public loans, the consequent outflow of bullion amounted to 17,000,000 yen. If matters were to continue in that way, the 'gold and silver reserves of our country will evaporate within ten years or so'. The same advocates also claimed that in the old days European countries levied protective tariffs and that the United States still did so. For these reasons, they argued, there were no means left other than protective duties to maintain national strength under existing conditions. But, for Tsuda, all of these arguments were untenable: 'Most Western political economists, with hardly any exception, agree that protective duties do not protect but impoverish a nation by raising prices.' Needless to say, by 'most Western political economists' he meant the current orthodox school of economic liberalism.

He continues by saying that in the United States protective duties were advocated by many but that this was only because American industry was inferior to its European counterparts and for that reason 'prices of manufactured commodities cannot be as cheap in the United States as in Europe'. Even though it was as harmful to the nation there as anywhere else to levy high duties on imported commodities, their aim was to promote their own industry, so that the benefit thereby gained might be returned to the people sooner or later. However, there could be no comparison between America and Japan in their respective 'arts and industries'. Those in Japan were far behind those in America and were next to nothing in comparison with those in Europe. That was precisely why such enormous amounts of money were paid to Western employees in Japan. Thus, 'it goes without saying whether it is wise or silly to try to follow the American way in the present situation in which we are placed.'

Tsuda enumerates his reasons for opposing protective duties. First, under the current treaties Japan had no right of its own to tax imported commodities. Second, even in the case of such commodities as iron which incurred enormous carriage expenses, imports from Britain were much cheaper than home products owing to the great difference in manufacturing arts. Third, even if taxes could be levied on Western wares which had already become necessities of life, the fact remained that there was no home industry to be protected by those taxes. Fourth, there was no point in preventing Western commodities from reaching the nation, because it was the manner of the age for the people to love things Western. Fifth, in the study of Western civilization the Japanese nation was practically at the stage equivalent to primary school, and the university stage was still far in the future. It was only to be expected that 'Japan should pay a large sum for tuition fees without immediately gaining from it'. The gap between imports and exports would simply keep growing.

Would the gold and silver reserves of the nation, therefore, not drain away before too long? Tsuda's attitude is quite optimistic and his answer echoes the response given by Sir Dudley North two centuries before him:

> There is nothing to worry about. Imports and exports are reciprocal. Sometimes the former may exceed the latter, but sometimes the balance swings the other way round. Just like heat and cold or ebb and flow, they fluctuate and thereby tend towards equilibrium.

No explanation is given as to why exports and imports tend to balance each other. Perhaps the implication is that economic affairs are, just like natural phenomena, regulated by one and the same principle of nature. It may have been reasonable for him to assert, as he did, that under the current conditions, with no autonomy in taxation, it was unrealistic to advocate protective duties, but it was certainly not logical to say that because Japan had no autonomy in tariffs, free trade was tenable. Probably his main point was his belief in the naturalistic view of the economy. He continues:

> How can the balance between exports and imports be recovered? There are only two ways, that is to say, either by an increase in exports or by a decrease in imports. For a few years after the opening of our ports exports exceeded imports, and for the next few years imports have exceeded exports. For another few years to come, exports will probably be in excess. Thus imports and exports circulate according to the law of nature and never fail to tend towards equilibrium. Arts and industry grow in the meantime, so that there is nothing to fear at all.

It is one thing, however, to say that in the long run imports and exports are regulated by the 'law of nature' and 'never fail to tend towards equilibrium', but it is entirely another to say that Japan is at the stage of learning a great deal from the West and so is obliged to pay a 'tuition fee' and that 'the balance between imports and exports will continue to grow according to the growth of the nation's accumulation of knowledge'. It also contradicts his own assertion, already quoted, that 'for another few years to come, exports will probably be in excess'.

Tsuda seems not to have realized this contradiction. In his article

'Boeki Kenkoron' (On the Balance of Trade), published in the following year, the arguments are essentially the same. The aim of the article, he writes, is to argue that the excess of imports should give rise to satisfaction rather than concern. The situation is caused by a national trait, peculiar to the Japanese, which is to welcome and learn about novel things. This is nothing less than 'a natural talent which encourages human industry and promotes human welfare', and 'is what differentiates our nation from the savage tribes in America or Africa'. It is this alone which has caused the excess of imports over exports. Imports range from 'railways, the telegraph, lighthouses, arms, mints, docks and all other apparatus' to 'tables and like utensils, cake, wine, and other similar foods' of the West.

Tsuda's firm belief in enlightenment is evident when he thus contrasts civilized with uncivilized states and goes on to claim that the imbalance between imports and exports should be welcomed and not lamented. Repeating the arguments propounded in the previous article, that foreign trade is controlled by the same law as that of the wind or of the tide, which always tend towards eventual equilibrium, he says that the balance between imports and exports should cause no concern to any patriot. However, his reasoning is now more overtly economic:

> Although the increase in imports results from our people's inclination to love new and pretty things, the difference between imports and exports is now too great, deviating so much from natural equilibrium that the quantity of imported foreign goods exceeds the purchasing power of the people. That is why Western commodities have fallen in price, sometimes well below their original cost. No doubt, this year, exports and imports will recover their natural balance or perhaps exports will exceed imports to compensate for last year's imbalance. Unless exports and imports balance each other, foreign trade will not last long.

Thus he explains how the increase in imports has caused an excess of supply over demand and consequently a fall in the price of imported goods, which in turn will cause a decrease in supply, and so produce equilibrium between supply and demand or a change-over from an unfavourable to a favourable balance of trade. The aforesaid 'law of nature' may be said now to have received a theoretical economic endorsement.

Ushiba Takuzo at once took up his pen to contradict this argument, saying that the reason for concern was not the imbalance between imports and exports as such but its inevitable outcome. As their friend Kanda Takahira said,[17] the imbalance would sooner or later drain away gold and silver reserves and thereby make paper money 'a piece of wasted paper', the consequence being that 'business would stop, manufacturing would decay, farming would be deserted, mines would close . . . and the people would suffer most'. Ushiba went on to say that free traders claimed that imports and exports would come to balance each other in the long run and that home industry would prosper with no need of protection, but 'when does the time really come?'[18] What Ushiba implies here is that the time might indeed come eventually, as Tsuda claimed, when the trade balance was brought to equilibrium, but that the national economy would already have been ruined before that time was reached.

In this way Tsuda's attitude towards contemporary problems, although within the inevitable bound of the Meiji Enlightenment, was that of a liberal political economist. His approach to practical policy problems was of that kind because his firm conviction in natural liberty at a more general level supported it. He writes: 'What is called law in the humanities and the science of political economy originates mostly in imagination. If a law clearly corresponds to the actual facts, then it is proved to be an inevitable law of nature. If not, it is simply a presumption.'[19] What, then, is that 'inevitable law of nature' in political economy? It is 'the nature of freedom' or 'self-interest'. Needless to say, there are evils attached to freedom. 'The right of freedom is a right inherent to everyone, a right which is esteemed most by all civilized nations. But no one is justified in abusing it by interfering with others' freedom.'

Tsuda believed that it was because only the unfavourable consequences of liberty had been taken into consideration that liberty had for so long been regarded as a vice in Japan. The result was that the natural freedom of humanity had been distorted and suppressed, and the mentality of the people had fallen into a mean and slavish state. Likewise, human love of profit had its merits as well as demerits. 'Self-interest' also had its positive as well as its negative side. 'Self-interest' was the propensity that people had for increasing their physical well-being, but it had an evil tendency as well towards avarice and stinginess – faults which had to be detected. On the other hand, it was wrong to look only at the negative side, as Confucians had tended to do, without paying due attention to the positive side. They had always taught moral virtues but not political economy, with the consequence that 'our people generally suffer poverty and lack physical happiness'. It was not understood that self-interest and natural order were not necessarily in contradiction to each other; on the contrary, self-interest did belong to the natural order of things.[20] Here we see that Tsuda's view of the traditional or orthodox conservative school of Confucianism is just like that of Nishi and Fukuzawa.

Thus, to Tsuda, political economy meant a science which could emancipate human nature from traditionally Confucian suppression. The background to all of his thinking lay in the experience he had had of learning at first hand the systematic political economy of the West.

Political economy was one of the five subjects, as we have already seen, that he learned from Professor Simon Vissering of the University of Leiden, Holland, where he, together with Nishi, was sent to study by the Shogunate government. While the lecture notes on jurisprudence and statistics were translated into Japanese by themselves and their friend Kanda after their return home, the notes that they had taken at Leiden on political economy were lost in one of the military conflicts between the Shogunate and anti-Shogunate forces. However, one might easily guess what Vissering's lectures in political economy were like from his book *Handboek van Praktische Staathuishoudkunde* (1862–5). Nishi writes that the book was composed of four volumes, the last of which had not yet been completed during their stay there. It seems, according to Nishi, that Vissering lectured without notes, picking up essential points from his book as he went along. In order either to announce his devotedness to J. B. Say's creed or merely to suggest the contents, Vissering quoted on the reverse of the title page of his book Say's words:[21] 'Ces principes ne sont point l'ouvrage des hommes; ils derivent de la nature des choses; on ne les établit pas: on les trouve' (*Traité d'Economie Politique*, first edn, 1803).

4

THE ECONOMIC THOUGHT OF FUKUZAWA YUKICHI

For the student of the history of modern Japan the name Fukuzawa Yukichi is inseparably fused with the epoch of the so-called Meiji Enlightenment. Indeed he contributed more than anybody else to the introduction to Japan of the ideas and benefits of Western civilization and he deserves the name of being a champion of the Enlightenment in Japan. He founded Keio School, which later developed into Keio University. He was one of the founders of the first business school in the country, which was to evolve into Hitotsubashi University, and also of the first limited company, which was the precursor of the Maruzen Company, as we shall see later in Chapters 5 and 6. As a writer on economic and other subjects, he was clearly ahead of his contemporaries and so deserves the greatest attention.

He has long been regarded as a liberal in his economic as well as political thought. While some people believe that he remained a liberal throughout his life, others claim that, in his writings published around 1880 (e.g. *Tsuzoku Kokkenron* [Popular Theory of the State's Rights] and *Jiji Shogen* [Current Affairs Briefly Discussed]), he switched from being a liberal to a nationalist and reverted to liberalism only towards the later period of his active life. The aim of the present chapter is to assess the real nature of his economic thought.

An episode from the period of political upheaval towards the end of the Tokugawa feudalist or Shogunate regime highlights the character of Fukuzawa. Despite the sound of gunfire close at hand, he carried on with his lecture in political economy at his private school in Tokyo, telling his apprehensive students that the future of the country had already been settled and that a little turmoil here and there was not worth bothering about. His was the first economics course ever given in any Japanese educational institution. The textbook that he used at the time was Francis Wayland's *The*

Elements of Political Economy (1837), about which he recollected some ten years later:

> It was one of those which I had never before come across. At first I found it hard just to follow the sentences, but after getting used to it by reading it twice or thrice, I was so deeply impressed by every chapter or even by every phrase, with its arguments and expressions so completely fresh to me, that I often forgot about having meals.[1]

For some unknown reason, Fukuzawa's course of lectures in political economy lasted for only a year, after which it was taken over by his ex-student and colleague Obata Tokujiro, who later translated the Wayland textbook into Japanese. Instead, Fukuzawa started lecturing on Wayland's *The Elements of Moral Science* (1844) in his class and never resumed lecturing in political economy.

Although Wayland is recognized as belonging to the second generation of the liberal school of political economy, Fukuzawa was, not only in his lecturing but also in his writing, one of the first to introduce political economy of the liberal school into Japan. In the year before the Meiji Restoration, he published a book entitled *Seiyo Jijo Gaihen* (Conditions in the West, vol. 2), which was a translation of the first part of a book issued by the Edinburgh publishing firm of William and Robert Chambers under the title *Chambers's Educational Course: Political Economy, for Use in Schools, and for Private Instruction*.[2]

Since, according to Fukuzawa, the latter half of the Chambers's book was more or less similar in content to a book already translated into Japanese by his friend Kanda Takahira, Fukuzawa refrained from translating that part. Kanda's translation was from the Dutch version of William Ellis's *Outlines of Social Economy* (1846). Setting aside the question of the extent to which the latter half of Chambers's *Political Economy* is similar to Ellis's book, here we see Fukuzawa's attitude towards what he believed to be the immediate priorities of the day; an attitude which alone might well earn him the name of being a champion of the Japanese Enlightenment.[3] He was determined to devote time and energy only to those matters that he considered to be essential.

In similar vein, Fukuzawa said that, when translating a Western book, there was no need to bother about elegance of style or phraseology; it was sufficient to concentrate on producing a plain and readable translation. He even said that, with the number of people able to read Western books believed to be increasing steadily day by day, the translation on which he was currently engaged would necessarily soon prove to be no more than elementary nonsense. Here, too, as described in more detail in the Appendix, it is clear that Fukuzawa made it a priority to meet the urgent task of enlightening people about the fruits of Western civilization.[4]

The first half of the Chambers's book, which he translated, is about social economy, whereas the second half, which he left untranslated, concerns political economy itself. The translation covers the following chapters: Social Organization; The Family Circle; Individual Rights and Duties; Civilization; Equality and Inequality; Distributions of Rank; Society as Competitive System; Divisions of Mankind into Nations; Intercourse of Nations with Each Other; Origins of Government; Different Kinds of Government; Laws and National Institutions; Government Functions and Measures; The Education of the People; The Nature of Political Economy; The Origin and Nature of Property; The Protection of Property; Protection of the Profits or Fruits of Property. The chapter on 'Objections to the Competitive System Considered' was omitted by Fukuzawa.

In addition to this material, Fukuzawa selected items from a few other sources and translated them. One of the additions is a chapter entitled 'Different Forms of Human Industry', from Francis Wayland's *The Elements of Political Economy*, in which the author refers to patent and copyright as a necessary protection for the results of mental labour which, unlike manual labour, is not remunerated according to its quantity. Both patent and copyright were as yet entirely unfamiliar to the Japanese readers but Fukuzawa believed them to be essential to the modernization of the country. This conviction may possibly have been backed by personal experience, since he himself had suffered from the absence of copyright. His *Seiyo Jijo, Shohen* (Conditions in the West, vol. 1), published the previous year, had been so warmly received by readers that many versions of it were printed and circulated without his permission.

Other additions were chapters on the life and work of James Watt and George Stephenson, who Fukuzawa apparently believed to be of particular importance. They, as well as Richard Arkwright and James Hargreaves, were named in the chapter on 'Society as a Competitive System' as examples of those who contributed to the wealth of society by profiting themselves.

The additions that Fukuzawa made seem quite understandable but why did he omit the one original chapter? In that chapter the author refers to the assertion that 'a much better condition of society would be produced by doing away altogether with individual emulation and competition, and establishing in their stead an associative system',[5] since 'the principle of competition and individual effort' is founded on the 'supposition that all men are sufficiently able by their mental and physical abilities . . . to realize the means of a comfortable livelihood', but the author is convinced that such is far from the case.[6] Although the source is not given, it was most probably taken from John Stuart Mill's *Principles of Political Economy*, Book 4, Chapter 7. In any case, the argument corresponds with the content of a chapter named 'Effects of a Partition of Property', which was the point at which Fukuzawa stopped translating. In this chapter 'a French writer of celebrity' is referred to as one who 'proclaimed the principle that property is robbery'. Here again the name of that writer is not explicitly mentioned, but it is obvious that it is the assertion of P. J. Proudhon that is implied. The author justifies the existing system of society, saying that such an assertion is simply 'empty speculation', since the partition of property can be achieved only by violence, which inevitably does away with capital and hence civilization.[7]

Thus one of the characteristics of this book is its advocacy of the capitalist regime of private property. To Fukuzawa, or rather to the Japan of his day, the capitalist society of the West seemed to represent civilization itself, which was the goal to be reached at any cost. Consequently any kind of antithesis to capitalism made no practical sense and so there was good reason for Fukuzawa to skip over that chapter.

There is, however, one other reason which makes his omission of interest. The author, in defence of the existing system against the 'Objections to the Competitive System', assumes that it has existed since the origin of human society, which fact proves that it suits human nature:

> We are endowed with ambition, emulation, the desire to improve our circumstances, and to engage in enterprises suitable to our individual tastes and capacities. . . . Political economy has proved that these instincts are highly beneficial to the community as well as to the individual; that they stimulate the activity and industry which increase the general wealth, and supply motives for the defence and preservation of that which industry has realized; and this, as far as we can judge, much

more effectively than would be the case if the interests were general instead of individual.[8]

This is nothing but a recitation of the old belief in natural freedom and pre-established harmony. One of the reasons why Fukuzawa spared himself the trouble of translating this chapter is very probably that he had no sympathy for these ideas and so felt no urge to translate this part.

This very lack of sympathy for, or conviction in, such social philosophy must certainly have made his economic liberalism less consistent than, for instance, that of Taguchi's. Conversely, it could have made his economic thought more realistic than Taguchi's.

There is something of the kind in some of the chapters that Fukuzawa did translate. In the chapter on 'The Nature of Political Economy', the point is made that 'it is not a system for controlling men's actions, but for discovering how men are induced by this natural propensity to act',[9] and that 'certain propensities [are] implanted in mankind, which, when viewed alone, have a selfish, narrow, and almost degrading aspect, are, when contemplated in relation to each other, a wise provision for enabling man to advocate his own welfare, happiness, and virtue.'[10] In the chapter on 'Government Functions and Measures' it is also said that 'it [government] cannot provide for the subsistence of the people at large; for the extent of the remuneration which workers should receive for their labour, or the extent to which they should work for the wages they obtain; for the extent to which commodities of any kind – such as food, clothing, &c. – should be procured, the manner in which they should be sold, or the price that should be paid for them; generally speaking, government should not interfere with trade.'[11] However, these statements carried much less weight than those parts that were omitted.

Thus, the greater part of the text which deals with political economy was deliberately omitted from *Seiyo Jijo, Gaihen* (Conditions in the West, vol. 2) and, in the little that was translated, the passage in which special stress is laid on natural liberty and pre-established harmony was dropped. What about Fukuzawa's own writing? What were his views there?

Fukuzawa did emphasize human equality, as is shown in the opening passage of the first book of *Gakumon no Susume* (An Encouragement of Learning): Heaven made humans so that no one is over or under another and no one is born nobler or meaner than another.[12] When comparing this with the first passage of the chapter on 'Individual Rights and Duties' in *Seiyo Jijo, Gaihen*, it is easy to see the influence that the Chambers's text had upon Fukuzawa because it runs:

> While God has given man the gift of life, he has also given him the capacity to support that life. . . . Accordingly, every human being, of whatever race or country, has, by a law of nature, the property of his own person. . . . This freedom he is not at liberty to sell or assign.[13]

Starting from this point, *Seiyo Jijo, Gaihen* (i.e. *Chambers's Educational Course*) proceeds to people's equality before the law and ends at their duty to obey the law. The same assertion regarding the duty to obey the law is also made in *Gakumon no Susume*, but the significance of this book lies in its encouragement of real learning, as against vain learning, for the reason that the inequality in wealth and intellect that exists among people in spite of their natural equality is caused by some being educated and others not. Also, based on the analogy of the equality of people at birth (Book I, 1872 and Book II, 1873), it proceeds to the equality of nations (Book III, 1873) in the following way:

> We have said in Book II that all men, whether rich or poor, whether physically strong or weak, are equal in their own right and that the same applies to the relation between people and government. Now in the present book [Book III] let us expand this principle to the discussion of the relation between nations.[14]

That is to say, as every individual is by nature equal with all others, so is every nation. Therefore, he argues:

> To defend our country against foreign countries it is essential to fill the whole country with the spirit of freedom and independence, and to let everyone, regardless of the difference in rank or wealth or knowledge, think of one's country as one's own interest and do one's duty to one's own nation. . . . To sacrifice one's property or even one's life for the sake of one's country: such is real loyalty.[15]

In Book X (1874) the independence of individuals is once again related to the independence of the nation by using the same level of logic:

> The phrase 'freedom and independence' is bound to imply the notion of duty. Independence does not mean merely non-reliance on others for the subsistence of life. It is more than an inner duty. There is an outer duty just as well, that is to say, the duty to exert oneself together with the rest of one's nation to make certain that one's country retains the state of freedom and independence. Only by so doing can it be said that one has performed one's duty in both ways.[16]

In a feudal society there was no choice of profession. But now:

> It is up to us all to choose whatever profession we wish. One can be a farmer, or a trader, or a scholar, or a civil servant, or a writer, or a journalist, or a lawyer, or an artist, or a manufacturer, or a statesman or anything else. All varieties of profession are open to free competition, but the competition is not for the sake of fighting against each other. On the contrary, the object of fighting, if not with one's sword but with one's intellect, is to confront foreigners. If we win in this intellectual fighting, then we shall improve the station of our country. If we lose, then we shall see it degraded.[17]

The aim of civilization is thus said to be 'to wage intellectual battle' against foreigners and to let one's own country surpass foreign countries. 'Peace inside and emulation outside', to be formulated later in *Jiji Shogen* (Current Affairs Briefly Discussed, 1881), is already clearly expressed here. Nationalism is evident throughout.

The same thing is shown even more clearly in *Bunmeiron no Gairyaku* (An Outline of a Theory of Civilization, 1875) where Fukuzawa claims to make European civilization the object of all his arguments[18] and yet, without pursuing the object for its own sake, makes the independence of the country the ultimate aim for which the civilizating of the nation should be the means.[19]

Such nationalism originates in his conception of the international circumstances of his time. Giving an example from India and Turkey, he says in Gakumon no Susume, Book XII (1874):

> When we look at India and Turkey, we cannot fail to admit that the former is a country well known for its literature and the latter is a great country of warriors. And yet, when we see how they are now, we find the one possessed by Britain and its people her slaves. Their sole business is to grow opium ... which British merchants sell at a great profit. Turkey is an

> independent country in name only whose trade is governed by the British and French. Its natural growth is obliged to decay every day by virtue of free trade ... and for manufactured commodities it is entirely dependent on imports from Britain and France. Its brave warriors in their poverty can hardly perform anything worthwhile. Why is it, then, that Indian culture and Turkish bravery have contributed little to their own civilization? ... It is because their outlook is confined within their own country without ever reaching outside.... They either enjoy peace at home or fight each other inside their own domain, while foreigners have been profiting from them by means of business and trade. Western merchants have not a rival within Asia, a fact of which we have to be well aware. If we are to fear these strong opponents and at the same time to admire their civilization, we must exert ourselves, comparing the circumstances inside with those outside.[20]

It is remarkable that the concept of developed countries controlling underdeveloped countries by means of free trade, or 'free trade imperialism' as the historians of economic thought now refer to it, is clearly anticipated here. However, Fukuzawa is not discussing the theory or policies of free trade or protection here. In Book XV (1876) he writes: 'Most British political economists favour free trade and those who believe in it maintain it as if it were a universal law which applies everywhere, whereas some American political economists argue for protection in their own way.'[21] Here again, however, he does not aim to contrast the one with the other in order to examine them both, because he continues to say simply that they are contradicting each other without ever coming to a conclusion. Instead, he aims to show the difference between the people in Western countries who tend to seek the truth of things by arguments and discussions and those in Asiatic countries who tend to stick to traditional silly prejudice, holding to the sayings of the ancient sages. To compare the rational with the irrational, the civilized with the uncivilized, is his aim. In *Gakumon no Susume* his interest does not extend to political economy as such, and there is a marked similarity to his attitude in *Seiyo Jijo, Gaihen*, where he deletes almost all of the parts dealing with political economy.

Thus, one of the main purposes of *Gakumon no Susume* is to stress the necessity of learning about Western civilization in order to confront Western countries. 'To fear and admire', that is to say, 'to fear strong opponents and at the same time to admire their civilization' is the attitude prevailing in many of his writings about that time. For example, in 'Nakatsu Rubetsu no Sho' (Farewell to Nakatsu), written in the same year as Seiyo Jijo, Nihen (1870), he writes:

> Since our foreign trade has started, there are many among the foreigners who want to enrich themselves by keeping us poor and ignorant. Therefore it would only serve to please foreigners if we were to continue to engage our interest in outdated Japanese and Chinese classics, preferring old fashion to new, and thus falling into a state of poverty and ignorance without acquainting ourselves with circumstances in the outer world. What they fear at this moment is our turning to Western studies. The way to achieve greatness for our country is to become acquainted with the world situation by reading as many Western books as possible, . . . to achieve the people's independence and liberty inwardly by acquiring knowledge and virtue, and to attain our nation's independence outwardly by keeping international laws.[22]

In *Keimo Tenarai no Bun* (Enlightening Penmanship, 1871) Fukuzawa also writes: 'Europeans are just the same human beings as we are, and so are Americans. Nothing can contribute more to the wealth and strength of the country than to study while young.'[23] In 1873, when he divided the classes at Keio School into two different courses, regular and short, he gave the reason for starting the latter course, as a wish to 'spread Western civilization rapidly in the country by reading, lecturing, or translating the books of the West, and thereby to increase the national strength'.[24]

Even though the independence of the country is set as one of the main aims, it does not imply that the independence of the individual is absorbed in the process merely as a means for achieving that goal. The shining spirit of enlightenment in its criticism of feudalism pervades the whole of *Gakumon no Susume*. Book I states that 'all men are born equal'. Book II asks: 'Is it not unreasonable that in feudal ages the division of classes between *samurai* and all other commoners was such that *samurai* treated the commoners as though the latter were criminals?'[25] Book VIII ponders: 'Is it not too partial and unfair a teaching for a book called *Onna Daigaku* (The Great Learning for Women) to preach three kinds of female obedience, first to parents, second to husband, and third to children?'[26] And the same question is raised in Book XIII:

> Once Confucius said, with regret, that women and the small-minded are unmanageable. . . . But men and women are not different by nature. . . . The noble and the common are also born equal. Why is it, then, that women and the small-minded are particularly vulnerable? Is it not unreasonable to say that they are hopelessly vulnerable after teaching them nothing but obedience and servility?[27]

On the other hand, it is characteristic of Fukuzawa that, as noted above, the independence of individuals is directly tied to the independence of the country. The following passage in Book I summarizes his logic:

> Both an individual and a country are free and independent by the law of nature. Therefore, if there should ever be a country which tries to interfere with the freedom of another, the latter ought to be brave enough to fight against that or any other country in the world. Likewise, if there should ever be any government officers who try to interfere with the freedom of a person, that person ought not to refrain from resisting.[28]

The logic with which the independence or equality of an individual and of a country is paralleled and combined on the same level was applied by Fukuzawa to his discussion of civic and national rights. With Fukuzawa it is not necessarily the case that by civic rights is meant the people's rights against the state, or by the state's rights the right on the part of the state to regulate people's inherent rights, and consequently that both kinds of rights are in conflict. It is true that there was such a view of the conflicting relationship between the people's and the state's rights when he said in *Bunmeiron no Gairyaku* that 'though the strong claim for the state's existence appears to be unfavourable to civic rights, it is of great use for establishing the authority of government and administration', and that 'though the unreserved argument for civic rights appears harmful to the security and maintenance of the peace of government, it is quite convenient for the abolishing of people's inherited attitude of servitude.' In the same way, he says in the preface to *Tsuzoku Kokkenron* (Popular Theory of the State's Rights, 1878) that he feared that he might be misunderstood by the reading public if he discussed the people's rights only without discussing the state's rights and that that was why he had postponed the publication of *Tsuzoku Minkenron* (Popular Theory of People's Rights, 1878) which he had already completed.[29] Then again it was his belief that 'to maintain the people's rights inside is in order to establish the national rights outside' and that 'therefore the people's rights and the state's rights are inseparable from each other'.[30] Here it is clear that by the state's rights is meant its rights against other states rather than against its own people,[31] so that the relation between the people's rights and the state's rights in this context is the same as that between personal independence and national independence, which was developed in another context in *Gakumon no Susume* as seen above. In *Tsuzoku Kokkenron* Book II (1879) Fukuzawa says that 'nothing is more urgent than letting all of the people of the country understand what the international circumstances now really are',[32] an undertaking which was succeeded in *Jiji Shogen* (Current Affairs Briefly Discussed, 1881) by his declaration that it was to be his 'life-long purpose' to 'improve the national rights'.[33]

In the meantime there was a heated controversy about the travel and residence of foreigners in Japan. As already noted in the preceding chapters, some people argued for the freedom of foreigners to travel and reside wherever they liked. Others were against this and argued that foreigners should be allowed to live only in a certain limited area. Fukuzawa was of the latter opinion. Referring to the problem, he wrote in *Bunkenron* (Decentralization of Power, 1877) that if free travel and residence were to be granted to foreigners, as he believed was inevitable sooner or later, 'the Japanese could not fail to be placed under their control because the foreigners are enlightened and skilled, whereas the Japanese are unenlightened and unskilled.'[34] Here, too, he lays the blame for local problems on the international circumstances in which Japan stopped its isolationist policy and opened itself to the outer world. During the period of isolation, he argues, people had only to trust the government with everything and to obey its instructions, but 'now that international communication has started, we have had to fight against foreigners in trade and industry, in science and arts, and in all other spheres'. It was a battle not merely between governments but between peoples. 'A step backward on our part necessarily means a step forward on their part.'[35] What he was discussing in this context was the need for the decentralization of power, but his real purpose lay rather in accustoming people to public affairs, and consequently foreign affairs, because he says: 'Decentralization of power can be said to be the way to train people for foreign intercourse. This is why I claim that it is high time for tackling the problem of the decentralization of power.'[36] Thus, even the argument for decentralization of power was put forward within the context of international relations, about which Fukuzawa was so concerned.

A similar argument to that in *Bunkenron* is found in volume 2 of *Minkan Keizairoku* (Popular Political Economy), which appeared three years later in 1880. Referring to railways as a significant element of civilization, in the chapter entitled 'On Transport', Fukuzawa writes that 'civilization and culture consist in the human control of nature' and that the 'convenience or inconvenience of transport depends on how skilfully or unskilfully the control of nature by human art has been achieved'. He maintains:

> There would have been no problems if it were still the age of isolation, as it was until twenty years ago. Now that we have opened our country and resumed the intercourse with foreigners, we are in an entirely different situation. We are no more than crawling worms, whereas they have wings to fly with. How can we rival them with their industry and trade, with their forces and tactics? We have never been in greater danger. This is why the construction of railways is now such an immediate necessity.[37]

Liberals such as Taguchi would have argued in a different vein that railways, like all other things, should be left alone so that they could be constructed when the time was ripe.[38]

Although both volumes of *Bunmeiron no Gairyaku* clearly show traces of what Fukuzawa learned from the popularized versions of classical political economy of Chambers and Wayland, his nationalism is nevertheless evident. In *Jiji Shogen* he goes one step further. He argues that Japan should rely only on the power of arms in order to compete with Western nations in the current world arena, and says that the motto 'wealth and strength' implies not the enrichment of the country first and the strengthening of arms next but the reverse, because without strength there cannot be wealth.[39] 'Can any country other than Japan among the Eastern countries be the centre of civilization with which to confront Western countries?' Therefore, he claims, 'Japan should be pursuaded that the defence of Asian countries is its responsibility.' Comparing defence to fire prevention, he continues:

> It is like the spread of fire when Western countries force themselves on us Eastern countries. The Eastern nations,

> particularly the Chinese and Koreans, are so slow and dull that they are no more capable of stopping the Westerners than wooden houses are able to withstand the force of fire. Therefore it is not merely for the sake of others but for our own sake that we must help them militarily. We must strive to protect them with force of arms and to lead them by cultural example, so that they too may enter the sphere of modern civilization. And, if there is no alternative, we may forcibly urge them to progress.

Indeed, he goes as far as to affirm that to 'forcibly urge them to progress' can be justified.[40]

In short, Fukuzawa regards international relations at large as consisting in 'the difference in magnitude and strength of financial and military power between the nations concerned'.[41] He asserts that 'one ought to be convinced that the essence of international intercourse consists in power'.[42] 'Peace inside and emulation outside' must be the only conclusion. Here again he believes that 'the reason why Japan is in need of peace inside arises solely from the opening up of the country some twenty years ago'.[43] The international circumstances (or, as one might put it, the imperialistic world situation of the time) in which Japan was obliged to open itself to the outer world influenced the early thinking of Fukuzawa throughout the period leading up to *Jiji Shogen*. Thus he regards an individual as being not an individual as such but always a member of the nation and consequently love of the nation as being paramount over self-love. In *Gakumon no Susume* he clearly states:

> Those who exert themselves to extend the right of their own nation, to enrich their own nation, to improve the wisdom and virtue of their own nation, and to glorify the honour of their own nation are called people faithful to their country. . . . Their aim must be to distinguish their country from others and to favour themselves in comparison with others, not necessarily to harm the latter but to retain the independence of their own country.[44]

This nationalism characterized Fukuzawa's notion of foreign trade as well. As has already been seen, the view that the choice between free trade and protection 'is simply dependent on the interest of one's own country' did not originate in *Jiji Shogen*. What prevails in the real world, he believes, is not 'natural freedom'. In the same section of *Bunmeiron no Gairyaku* he declares, 'The world as it presently stands may aptly be called the world of business and war.'[45]

As early as 1869, only two years after *Seiyo Jijo, Galhen*, he wrote in 'Maruya Shosha no Ki' (Prospectus of Maruya & Co.; see Chapter 6), 'It goes without saying that the principal aim of foreigners in meeting our compatriots . . . is nothing other than making a profit out of the latter by means of trade. Therefore it would be contrary to our duty as Japanese if we stood idly by while foreigners kept the right of business and trade in this country in their own hands.'[46] His view on foreign trade is exactly the same in the following year when he states in 'Nakatsu Rubetsu no Sho' that 'since our foreign trade has started, there are many among the foreigners who want to enrich themselves by keeping us poor and ignorant.'[47] This view is carried through to *Bunmeiron no Gairyaku* via 'Shogakko o tatsuru no Shui' (Prospectus of the School of Commerce, 1874), 'Seitai Wagi no Enzetsu' (Speech on the Peace of Taiwan, 1874) and 'Ajia Shokoku to no Wasen' (Peace or War with Asian Countries, 1875).

In 'Shogakko o tatsuru no Shui', as will be seen in more detail in Chapter 5, he regards 'waging the war of trade against foreign countries' as 'the public duty of merchants now' and says that 'in fighting one another by means of the sword one cannot go to the battlefield without learning the art of fencing beforehand'. Likewise, 'in the age of battles by means of business, one cannot be confronted with foreigners without learning the art of business in advance.'[48] In 'Seitai Wagi no Enzetsu' he warns that, although the reparations paid as a result of sending armies to Taiwan are welcome enough, it is important to consider more than just the two countries concerned. 'As to profit or loss, there are other parties too . . . Western countries. Although they are not directly involved in the war or peace between Japan and China, . . . they are concerned in it through trade.' Following the disputes, when Japan and China were trying to build up their stocks of armaments, 'the Westerners are the selling party and the Japanese and Chinese are the buying party', because 'nowadays all of the equipment, from warships, guns and artillery down to the clothes, shoes and hats which soldiers wear, is of foreign make. . . . It is the Western merchants who always gain and never lose.' It was true that 'a war is a matter of the honour or dishonour, rise or fall of the country concerned, and so it should not be regarded only from the viewpoint of mercenary gain or loss', but nevertheless 'we should be provident enough not to allow the Westerners to profit by the disputes between us Asians.' Thus, 'our present difficulties consist in international matters. Our powerful enemy now is in fact the Western countries. They are not an enemy in the military sense but in the trading sense.'[49]

His argument in 'Ajia Shokoku to no Wasen' is very much to the same effect. He is opposed to the Korean War because 'it would hardly be worth the rejoicing if Korea were to bring tributes and become our colony'. It would even constitute a loss to fight against the Koreans, since 'to win there would not bring us honour and it would be no benefit to us to occupy the country, because spending a huge sum of money in order to buy commodities, guns and artillery of Western make would only amount to an increase in our foreign debt.' He goes on to say that 'Japan will not achieve real independence unless it stands on an equal footing with Western countries', and that 'although there is foreign trade carried on in our major ports, all of it must be said to be in foreigners' hands'. Indeed, 'there are plans to start some manufacturing enterprises, but the fact is that the Japanese are always on the borrowing side of capital and never on the lending side.'[50]

As though to formulate these arguments in a conclusive way, he writes in *Bunmeiron no Gairyaku*:

> If one looks at the trade between Japan and foreign countries, one sees that Western countries are the manufacturers and Japan is the grower. . . . In economy the wealth of a nation depends far less on the surplus of natural produce than on the skill of human arts. For example, there is India, on the one hand, where land is fertile and yet people are poor, and there is Holland, on the other, where there is scarcely any natural produce and yet people are rich. Therefore in trade between a manufacturing country and a growing country, the former makes use of unlimited human power and the latter the limited produce of land. . . . This is exactly the case with the trade between Japan and foreign countries. We can only be on the losing side.[51]

Five years later, in 'Boeki Shokai Kaigyo no Enzetsu' (Opening Speech of a Trading Company) he says: 'When I look at the foreigners who have arrived by ship, who are selling their commodities to us and then buying our products to export, I cannot help saying that they are always the merchants and we are always the customers.' He continues:

> How do the foreigners live who reside in our trading ports? From where does their subsistence come? Riding beautiful

> horses, sitting in fabulous coaches, they spend millions or else take back the money to their home countries. That money . . . is nothing less than the outcome of the sweat of our brow. What else do we have to lament?

He even invokes the spirit of the exclusionists whom he used to loathe so much: 'The exclusionists of the old days wanted to resort to violence to expel from Japan foreigners whom they despised as lower creatures. The difference between them and us . . . lies only in that we want to fight in business and trade.' He goes on to say: 'Postponing a military battle with foreigners to some future day, at the moment we merely want to fight a trade battle.'[52] Although it might seem extraordinary to hear him refer to the exclusionists, the analogy of an armed conflict is not surprising, as must be clear enough already.

It would be strange if such a view of foreign trade did not result in balance-of-trade theory or protectionism. Indeed, that sort of theory may be said to be implied in these arguments. In the same year, 1875, as *Bunmeiron no Gairyaku*, he wrote for the periodical *Minkan Zasshi* an article called 'Gaikokujin no Naichi Zakkyo yurusu bekarazaru no Ron' (Foreigners should not be allowed to live freely among the Japanese), in which he revealed this view explicit. On that subject there was, as mentioned already, a series of heated arguments between some leading writers. Free-traders such as Nishi Amane and Tsuda Mamichi argued for the freedom of residence for foreigners, while protectionists such as Nishimura Shigeki and his friends argued against it.[53] Fukuzawa says:

> It is a great mistake to try to introduce Western civilization merely by permitting foreigners to travel and reside freely in our country, regardless of the unfavourable consequences that this would obviously bring about. . . . It is all too premature to permit it. . . . The urgent priority today lies inside rather than outside. For the time being we must nourish our people's minds and spirits until the time is ripe to let foreigners obey our laws on equal terms with ourselves, and only then ought their freedom of travel and residence be allowed.[54]

Since in practical terms the freedom to travel and to reside must also mean the freedom to trade, this conclusion implies an argument against free trade. In the course of discussion his anti-free trade stance is more clearly disclosed: 'Foreigners come to Japan for the purpose only of trade and not for imparting knowledge and virtue to the people of Japan and thereby leading them to civilization.' He admits that, since the opening of the country, 'we have made changes in a great many ways, abolishing the old and seeking the new, and have gone so far as to overthrow the feudal government'; this being the outcome of the intercourse with foreigners. But, for foreigners themselves, all of this is simply 'by chance' and not by design:[55]

> Foreign trade means that people inside and outside the country fight for profit, and the ports are the place where that fighting takes place. When we look at how the trade has been conducted, we cannot fail to realize that we have always been on the losing side and they have been on the winning side. Therefore we can only say that the growth of foreign trade until today has brought about a decrease rather than an increase in our wealth.[56]

He summarizes his ideas in a few points, of which the first two in particular express his views on trade:

1 When exports are small and imports are large in value, the balance between the two must be our debts.
2 Our imports are mostly manufactured commodities and our exports are natural produce. For that reason our nation will lose not only the advantages that accompany manufacturing industry but also the skill with which to produce manufactured commodities. This is undoubtedly a great barrier to the very source of wealth.[57]

This is simply the mercantilist balance-of-trade theory which ironically is the antithesis of the views, to which Fukuzawa once subscribed so earnestly, of Francis Wayland in his *Elements of Political Economy*:

> We see how fallacious is the notion formerly entertained that, by exchange, only one party is benefited; and consequently, that what one party gains, the other party loses. Were this the case, no country would grow rich by exchange, unless by impoverishing every other country; and the gain of one nation would be nothing else than a transfer of the wealth of other countries to itself. On the contrary, precisely the reverse is the case.[58]

Fukuzawa's claim is exactly to the contrary, since he states that, in trade, gain on one side is loss on the other, and that Japan has always been on the losing side. He says: 'What we lose must necessarily amount to what they gain. Therefore in trade foreigners have attained their objective of competing in order to make a profit, and we have lost what they have gained.'[59]

He cites the example of the export of gold coins for some time after the opening up of the country. If a merchant, he says, buys up gold coins worth 1,000 dollars for only 400 dollars and then sells them to foreigners for 600 dollars, he may indeed gain the balance of 200 dollars, but from the standpoint of the nation at large this transaction has resulted in the loss of 400 dollars. The same applies in the case of silk and tea. Since the opening of the country, the production of silk and tea has increased and their price has risen but it cannot be deemed to be a 'blessing of trade'. On the contrary, 'the fact is simply that their price has risen only in comparison to what it was previously'. From the viewpoint of the nation's foreign trade, that is to say, Japan's relationship to foreign merchants, all of the gain lies with the latter and not with Japan. Furthermore, 'our silk and tea are exported raw to be exchanged for their manufactured commodities. Worse still, it is often seen that they manufacture our raw silk and we import that manufactured silk cloth for our own use. . . . If in such a way our manufacturing trades should be lost to the foreigners' monopoly, our nation's basic riches would go West day after day, until the Japanese would eventually fall into the condition of labourers at their beck and call.'[60] Thus Fukuzawa describes the influence of the exportation of raw materials and the importation of manufactured commodities on the balance of trade, and consequently on the outflow of capital and the loss of employment.

Needless to say, the assertion made by Fukuzawa that Japan was obliged to be a loser in foreign trade does not mean that he suspected the benefit of foreign trade as such. His attitude towards it had not changed since 'Tojin Orai' (Foreigners In and Out) written about 1865, in which he stressed the need for the opening up of the country and for foreign trade. This belief was to become the foundation of his later economic thought. He did not specify any particular trade as favourable or unfavourable from the balance-of-trade point of view. What he meant here by foreign trade was simply trade with advanced countries at large. 'What foreign trade is to our country is as nutrition is to the human body', but 'though the benefit of nutrition cannot be denied, the physical conditions must first be questioned.' As the physical conditions are yet feeble, it is harmful to apply too much of a good medicine at a time. It is exactly the same with the country. 'Good medicine must be applied only little by little so that it can be gradually increased.'[61] Protection is the only reasonable policy that can be practised. He emphasizes the significance of foreign trade and at the same time asserts that free trade can hardly apply until foreign countries and Japan can stand on an equal footing.[62] In *Tsuzoku Kokkenron* in 1878 he expresses his opinion even more explicitly:

> Regarding foreign trade there is a theory that foreign commodities should be freely admitted into the country so that anything that is inexpensive might be bought and consumed. There is another theory that claims that, by importing manufactured commodities from abroad and exporting natural home produce, the nation cannot fail to lose the profit that would otherwise be gained by manufacturing the produce and will eventually lose the manufacturing art itself. . . . Therefore it is asserted that these imports should be either restricted or heavily taxed. I, for one, agree with this latter opinion but, because of the unequal treaties, there is no prospect yet of any restriction in trade being adopted.[63]

In *Jiji Shogen* he says that just as the theory of natural civil rights applies only in the ideal state 'where all men are brothers and have equal access to the gifts of nature', whereas in reality 'the theory of government established in every country . . . to keep peace inside' actually applies, so, between countries, the theory of 'mutual intercourse providing each with its own necessity', which is 'parallel to the above theory of natural freedom', is evidently at odds with, and amazingly far from, real international intercourse.[64] Likewise, he says that just as the international relationship in wartime entails 'fighting with weapons', so in peace time it means 'fighting with industry and trade'.[65] These are similar arguments to that in *Bunmeiron no Gairyaku*, six years earlier, in which he wrote:

> It is often asserted that 'international intercourse is based on the example set by nature, so that free trade and free traffic should be observed. . . . But in order that this might be true, the first priority is to abolish all of the governments of the world in the same way as each clan in feudal Japan was abolished at the time of the Meiji Restoration. . . . If there is no prospect of that, and if there continues to be a government in every country, then national feelings cannot be denied.'[66]

In short, he believes that free trade is good enough as an abstract theory but not applicable in reality.[67] In the same vein he refers to free trade and protection:

> In a country such as Britain, where there is a surplus of commodities manufactured by human art and exported with profit all over the world, free trade is defended by most scholars, whereas in a country such as America, where there are plenty of natural goods but not as yet many manufactured commodities, protection is defended. It is no wonder that the argument between both sides continues *ad infinitum*.[68]

Of significance here is not Fukuzawa's opinion as to which of the two theories is superior but his assertion that both free trade and protection are 'after all in the interest of their own country' and that protectionism in America was possible only because it was backed up by American military power, with the result that 'a mere country in Asia' would not be allowed by Western countries, even if it wanted, to levy 'extraordinary customs duties'.[69] The remark that 'extraordinary customs duties' would not be allowed corresponds with the quotation from *Tsuzoku Kokkenron*, cited above, concerning no prospect of any restriction in imports because of the unequal treaties with foreign countries. Fukuzawa's conception of trade, i.e. free trade for developed countries and protection for less developed countries, seems to be too clearly stated to leave any room for doubt.

Even so, it is hardly conceivable that in Fukuzawa's thinking, which was influenced at the start by the books of Chambers and Wayland, there is no element of economic liberalism, free trade apart. As early as 1871 he referred to political economy in *Keimo Tenarai no Bun* (Enlightening Penmanship). Enumerating the 'subjects of Western studies', such as mathematics, physics and history, he highlights political economy as 'the science which discusses the necessities of life, and also the way to produce, exchange, . . . and increase them'. By defining it as 'a science to make clear that, whether privately or nationally, those who follow the law of nature are enriched and those who do not are impoverished',[70] he seems to imply economic liberalism, though what the 'law of nature' means is not apparent as yet.

However, in *Bunkenron* (Decentralization of Power, 1877) there is a passage where he appears to defend government non-interference and freedom of competition:

> It must be admitted that those people who hold positions in the government at present, regardless of their present ranks and past careers, are more advanced in their knowledge and faculties than the rest of the nation. This being so, the more advanced

> ought to lead the less advanced.... On that very point, the government in Japan differs from those in Western countries, since it has, as it were, a private task to carry out besides its own official task.

Therefore 'to assert the theory of natural freedom and to accuse the government of busying itself with its many tasks while blindly listening to the abstract and vain theory of the West without considering the actual conditions of the country, is only idle speculation.' Yet, 'those who are in the government, however advanced they may be in abstract knowledge, are not as well acquainted with practical matters as the people at large.' Theory is one thing, while practical application is quite another. A designer of a ship is not a shipwright or a pilot. Pathology and a clinic are not the same.

> If the government, misunderstanding this and mixing up theory with practice, should try to act on practical matters, the evils accruing from its action would be countless. The government officers, who are all ex-*samurai*, are least acquainted with the practice of industry and trade. If they should happen to spend a vast amount of money, far greater than that from any other source, the result would most probably be plunder and waste.[71]

Thus Fukuzawa argued that the government should not be the agent of any economic activities. The current state of affairs, as he saw it, was that 'without depending on government aid, hardly any capital can be raised for trade and industry, and in many fields trade and industry have already been started by the government. Such is the case with the reclamation of waste land or the opening of the new mines.'[72]

This argument admittedly contains only a denial of the government's directly operating trade and industry. However, Fukuzawa also says that 'in an economy one spends only to gain'. On that point all people are the same, hence the competition among them all. 'They are all equally concerned with comparing expenditure with income, thus competing with each other on the prospect of being a winner.' On the other hand, the conduct of the government 'which spends without due consideration of gain' tends not only to be 'spendthrift and wasteful' but also to interfere with the mutual competition among individuals, thus resulting in 'double losses'.[73]

In this way Fukuzawa rejects the idea of the government's directly running business and at the same time presupposes the 'principle of competition'. Here also is implied the exclusion of the government from intervening in the national economy by means of prohibition, permission, protection and the like. In fact, Fukuzawa says, 'It would prove harmful and unprofitable for the government to intervene in practical affairs, either by encouraging and protecting, or by prohibiting them.'[74]

This accords with the definition that he gave of the duty of government, namely 'jurisprudence, military affairs, taxation and foreign intercourse', in the chapter 'On Government' in *Minkan Keizairoku*, which was published in the same year.[75] Although the context in which the definition is set deals directly with the division between central and local governments and does not positively limit the part to be played by the government, the duty of government is confined, albeit indirectly, to the above four items.

Something of a similar nature is found in *Minkan Keizairoku*, volume 2, published three years later. In chapter on 'Public Works' he writes that 'great public affairs', such as railways, telegraph, gas and water supplies, or, like iron mines, 'what does not directly relate to public affairs and yet costs too much to be run privately without loss and at the same time cannot be left undone for the nation', should be entrusted to the government. Then he continues:

> It would be a great mistake to misunderstand the principle and to believe that the government may do anything in order to enrich the nation, running ordinary works and even competing with people in industry and trade. Only competition can lead industry and trade to average prices and can induce in the parties concerned every exertion. If someone should do something without due consideration of profit or loss . . . the effect would be disastrous.

He gives an example in the Tokugawa period that, when some clans ran businesses of their own, 'there arose no great businessmen at all'.[76] Fukuzawa's assertion is that nothing ought to be run by the government except what is properly entrusted to it. Everything concerning trade and industry should be carried on solely on the basis of competition.

Protection is likewise criticized:

> If the government has not run any business of its own, it sometimes protects some people by lending them some of its

> money under the pretext of encouraging trade and industry which are important to the economy of the country. . . . But there can be no business whatsoever that is of no importance to the nation.[77]

In *Bunmeiron no Gairyaku* as well, Fukuzawa refers to government non-interference: 'In attaining civilization everyone has to do their duty. The government deals with current necessities, scholars consider the future, and people of industry and trade enrich the country through their own private business, all of them thus participating in civilization in their respective ways.' The main point of discussion in this passage is the relationship between the government and scholars, and not that between the government and industry and trade. Nevertheless it also implies that the government on the one hand and industry and trade on the other should fulfil their respective duties. With regard to the relationship between the government and the people, the book, in another context, also says that 'the government and the people differ from each other, so that the government ought never to meddle in private matters', and that 'it would be totally baseless' for the government to levy taxes to 'regulate the matter of religion and education, order the rules of industry and trade, and even go as far as to meddle in the daily affairs of private families'.[78] Again, although the main theme here is not the relationship of the government to trade, industry and agriculture in particular, it is evident that government interference in the economy is regarded as untenable.

When it is said that the duty of people of industry and trade is to enrich the country through their own private business, the philosophy of natural liberty or *laissez-faire* might seem to be suggested. Similarly, an article by Fukuzawa in *Minkan Zasshi* (Popular Magazine) two years later, in 1877, stating that 'private interest is the basis of public benefit, the latter of which can be attained only by those who pursue the former'[79] might also seem to support such an interpretation. However, it must be pointed out that the phrase 'public interest', as used by Fukuzawa, is not an abstract term but, on the contrary, quite clearly means national benefit. He states even more plainly in an article written in 1879, entitled 'Watakushi no Ri itonamubeki no Ichirei' (Private Interest should be Attained: an Example), that 'the private profit of each merchant will eventually be gathered and accumulated to contribute to Japan's victory in the business world'.[80]

It may safely be concluded, therefore, that Fukuzawa's economic thought clearly contains elements of economic liberalism, in the sense of independence from the government or government non-intervention, which nevertheless goes hand in hand with economic nationalism and, consequently, mercantilist protectionism.

5

THE BIRTH OF BUSINESS EDUCATION

The birth of business education in Japan represents a phase of the Japanese Enlightenment. The story starts with Mori Arinori, the first Japanese Ambassador to the United States of America. Mori is generally believed to have been a progressive liberal, one of the so-called champions of the Japanese Enlightenment who characterized the intellectual climate during the years following the end of the long-lived feudal regime. He became, as did many others, a reactionary nationalist later in life. Years later, when he was assassinated in 1899, a famous journalist named Tokutomi Soho wrote in his periodical *Kokumin no Tomo* (Friend of the Nation) that Mori had been extremely liberal and radical in the beginning but had become extremely conservative and despotic in the end.[1] Ironically, Tokutomi himself was later to become an ultra-nationalist.

With regard to enlightenment, Mori claimed that his mother tongue was too peculiar, too retarded and consequently not suitable for the reception of Western civilization and thereby for the modernization of his country. He believed that English, or rather what he conceived to be a more rationalized version of English, should be adopted as the new national language. Thus, implementing modernization through Westernization was the duty that he imposed upon himself. During his term as Ambassador at Washington DC, he wrote to a number of prominent Americans, asking for their advice about the line that Japan should follow with regard to education:

> In a general way, I wish to have your views with reference to the elevation of the education of Japan, intellectually, morally, and physically.

This phraseology suggests that Mori was even then familiar with some of Herbert Spencer's writings; 'even then', because it has recently been made known in an excellent work on Mori by I. P. Hall that Mori met Spencer regularly in the latter's favourite club, the Athenaeum, while Mori was posted in London as Ambassador to the United Kingdom.[2] His letter continues:

> but the particular points to which I invite your attention are as follows:
>
> The effect of education
> 1 Upon the material prosperity of a country
> 2 Upon its commerce
> 3 Upon its agricultural and industrial interests
> 4 Upon the social, moral, and physical condition of the people;
>
> and
>
> 5 The influences upon the laws and government.
>
> Information on any one, if not all, of these points will be gratefully received and appreciated.[3]

To this request some people answered briefly, others in detail. With regard to civil liberty, Mark Hopkins, President of Williams College, advised that 'freedom be allowed that is compatible with order, especially freedom of opinion and religious worship',[4] and G. S. Boutwell wrote that 'a system of education should not include the teaching of any particular dogmas or opinions in religion, and experience is calculated to strengthen this opinion'.[5] With regard to practical skills, Peter Cooper of New York stressed the need for polytechnic or adult schools where mechanics could acquire useful knowledge.

Of especial interest in the present context is the advice relating to political economy and commerce. To Mori this must have seemed quite relevant to the advice given on liberty and the stress laid on the need for practical knowledge as means of advancing the modernization of Japan. Professor J. H. Steele of Amhurst College pointed out:

> The production and accumulation of wealth follow great laws as exactly as do the movements of the tide and the planets. There is a science of public economy, that is, a science of wealth, as true and as beautiful as the science of astronomy. All the mistakes which governments have ever made in their financial legislation, or which individuals make in their business transactions, come from ignorance of the fundamental truths of this

> science. Knowledge of this, therefore, is all-important for any nation, but such knowledge is not easily gained. The science, though now in its main principles well established, is very intricate, and demands well-trained intellects to master it.

Steele no doubt believed in the natural freedom of classical political economy. He seems to be encouraging the launching of schools where 'well-trained intellects' can be fostered. He continued:

> From what I have already said the bearing of education upon commerce will appear. Education implies a knowledge of ourselves and of others. This implies a knowledge of our wants and how to supply them, and this is the foundation of trade. . . . It is always a healthy sign of individual or national growth, when we feel our wants, and thus recognize our dependence on others. Industry and commerce and wealth grow out of this and, therefore, for the sake of commerce I would say, make education thorough and universal.[6]

James McCosh, President of Princeton University, also referred to commerce, saying that 'commerce can be extensively carried on only in nations in which there is a body of enlightened mercantile men, who know the wants of the country, and the products to be had in other countries'.[7]

Joseph Henry also referred to political economy and commerce, saying that the former was an important subject which ought to occupy the attention of Japanese statesmen, and the basic principles of which ought to be taught in higher institutions of learning. He continued:

> Although there is scarcely any department of human thought which has been more obscured with sophism, there is in it a basis of established truths which is of the greatest value, especially to those who are to make laws which regulate the commerce of your country.[8]

A professor at Rutgers University, replying on behalf of the president, W. H. Campbell, touched on the first item in Mori's enquiry, saying:

> National prosperity is held to consist in the accumulation of wealth in the hands of the inhabitants, in the general activity of trade and exchange, in the increase of the productions of a country, and in its general growth in population. These circum-

stances, which constitute material growth, are sure evidence also of the existence of happiness and contentment among the people, and have no small share in producing them.... It [education] stimulates in the mind of the individual a desire to improve his present condition, and aids him in devising ways and means to do so.

Referring to the second of Mori's points, i.e. the effect of education on commerce, the professor stated:

> Commerce brings nations into relations with each other. The seclusion of an empire from the rest of the world not only narrows and represses the national character, but also, by its effect upon commercial relations, cuts it off from one of the chief sources of material wealth. In order that these relations be mutually satisfactory and mutually advantageous, a common ground of intelligence and culture must exist between them.... It is, however, the work of time, and in that work education must be a principal instrument. It is that which must stimulate the national mind to strive after the advantages of commerce; and it is that alone which can train up a body of men fitted by knowledge, skill, and enterprise, to carry on its vast and far-reaching schemes.[9]

There is little doubt that Mori was deeply impressed by these answers. It may also be that he felt that his belief in the need for business education was confirmed and strengthened. In fact he already knew that there was a system of business education in the United States of America. In September 1871, in the introductory part of an English-language book published under the title *Life and Resources in America*, he had referred to the Bryant and Stratton College established in Chicago in 1856 and to a number of its branch colleges established thereafter in various parts of the country. The passage runs:

> In none of the public schools of America are the foundation principles of commerce taught, and hence there have been established by private individuals what is called a 'Chain of Commercial Colleges'; they number not less than forty, and extend from Maine to Louisiana; their course of instruction is very complete, and covers all that is necessary for commercial life.[10]

Mori became convinced that the wealth and strength of the United

States resulted from the richness of not only natural resources but also human resources. One conspicuous difference between America and Japan seemed to him to be the fact that, while in America people of ability were willing to engage themselves in business, in Japan education in business and trade had for so long been neglected or even despised. As we shall see later, this is exactly the view shared by Fukuzawa. Thus convinced of the urgent need for modernization in general, and for business education in particular, Mori returned to Japan in 1873. There he immediately initiated the enlightenment movement by, for instance, organizing a society called Meirokusha (Meiji Six Society) with its own journal *Meiroku Zasshi* (Meiji Six Journal). The establishment of a commercial school also had top priority.

He applied to the Tokyo Council for financial aid to employ a suitable American as a teacher, and also for a plot of land, rent-free, for the campus of his intended school. The Tokyo Council had succeeded the Tokyo Reconstruction Council established in 1872 in order to take charge of the Edo 7 per cent fund. This fund had originally been organized in 1791, following the deflationist policy executed by Matsudaira Sadanobu who was then in office under the Shogunate government. It was intended to defray the costs, both present and future, of natural disasters such as earthquake and great fire and was met by amassing 7 per cent of the total yearly rates of Edo (later to be renamed Tokyo after the Restoration). It was akin to the Sinking Fund that was much discussed in Britain in the late eighteenth and early nineteenth centuries. After the collapse of the Shogunate regime in 1868, there was no office responsible for the accumulated fund.

The Council, after a successful application to the Tokyo Prefectural Government, acceeded to Mori's request. Meanwhile, Mori invited Dr W. C. Whitney of the Newark branch of the abovementioned 'chain of commercial colleges' to teach at the school that he was to start. The appointment was made on the recommendation of the then acting Japanese Consul in New York Tomita Tetsunosuke (who was later to become the Vice-President of the Bank of Japan, and afterwards the Governor of Tokyo Prefecture), an ex-student of the Newark branch. Whitney arrived in Japan together with his family in August 1875 to take up the post. There seems to have been some misunderstanding between Mori and Whitney over the type of commercial education to be given in Japan, to which we shall return later.

Construction of the school, to be named Shoho Koshujo (Commercial Training School) was begun in a part of Tokyo called Tsukiji. However, without waiting for the completion of the building, the school itself started in the hall of a wholesaler's shop in neighbouring Ginza, in September 1875. This marked the beginning of commercial, or business, education in Japan generally and, in particular, the inauguration of a school which was eventually to develop into Hitotsubashi University. Today Ginza is reputedly the most fashionable part of the city. Owing to the rapid changes that have taken place there nothing now remains of the school except for an insignificant monument built by the alumini association of Hitotsubashi. On completion of the building in Tsukiji, the school moved to the new premises. Later the campus became too small to accommodate the increased number of students and staff, and so the school moved to yet another part of the city called Hitotsubashi. It stayed there until the great earthquake of 1923, when it had to move to a suburban part of Tokyo Prefecture. Thus, Hitotsubashi University, so named in the period after World War II, owes its name to the days when it was located in central Tokyo.

Fukuzawa Yukichi, on behalf of the three trustees of the school, namely Mori Arinori, Mitsukuri Shuhei and himself, wrote in the prospectus:

> In the past when Japan closed itself to the outer world, its merchants had only to be acquainted with inland trade, and it was sufficient for them to be smart enough not to miss any business chance there. . . . Now that foreign trade has begun, things have changed drastically. Until now the wealth or skill of a merchant has been only a private matter. Now he must recognize his public duty in knowing how to deal with Western merchants. . . . The extent of civilization within the country as a whole is such that any backwardness in business and trade cannot be criticized. Innovations cannot be brought in all at once. . . . In every Western country it has been recognized that where there are merchants, there are also commercial schools. Similarly in Japan in the feudal ages, where there were samurai, there were fencing schools. In fighting one another by means of the sword, one cannot go to the battlefield without learning the art of fencing beforehand. Likewise, in the age of battles by means of business, one cannot be confronted with foreigners without learning the art of business in advance.[11]

To claim that the object of a commercial school is to teach the would-be merchant how to fight against foreigners is nothing less than nationalism, or, it might be said, mercantilism. This is by no means extraordinary for Fukuzawa, even though he, as another champion of the Japanese Enlightenment, is so well known for his attitude towards introducing Western liberalism in all aspects of life, cultural, political, and economic, as we have already seen. Indeed, nationalism permeates all of his writing at that time. For example, in the translator's preface to the Japanese version of *Bryant and Stratton's Common School Bookkeeping*, which he had published two years previously, he wrote unequivocally:

> In Japan, since ancient times, the learned have always tended to be poor and the wealthy to be ignorant. The former are so proud of themselves and yet do not even know how to pay their own debts, whereas the latter are so humble as to regard all learning as irrelevant to their business. This arises from neither knowing that business and trade are the stuff of learning. If both were to come to know the truth of the matter, and if the learned should become wealthy and the wealthy learned through the study of this text on bookkeeping, then the economy of the whole nation might be completely reformed and the power of the country greatly increased. Nothing would please the present translator more.[12]

Here we see again that what mattered to Fukuzawa was 'the power of the country'. Another, and perhaps even more notable, example is his most famous work, *Gakumon no Susume* (An Encouragement of Learning). In the twelfth book of it, written only a few months before the prospectus, he presents very much the same view with reference to India and Turkey (see Chapter 4).

Two incidents, one involving Tomita, and the other involving Mori, illustrate the significance of nationalism. Years before, Tomita had been sent by his clan to study at the private school of Katsu Rintaro. (Katsu later achieved fame for the role he played, representing the Shogunate, in the negotiations with Saigo Takamori, representing the would-be Meiji government, which led successfully to the peaceful transfer of political power that was to become known as the Meiji Restoration.) In those days, when education was not yet officially institutionalized, it was quite usual for a cultured person to run a small-scale private school. Katsu sent his student Tomita to America to accompany his son whom he wanted to be enrolled as a student of the Naval Academy at Annapolis, Maryland. Katsu, who had once been the headmaster of the Shogunate's Naval Training School at Nagasaki, was firmly convinced that the future of Japan very much depended upon the development of a modern naval system. Tomita, hearing in America the news of the eventual collapse of the Shogunate regime, was worried about his master Katsu and about the fate of his parents and of the lord of his own clan at Sendai who had joined the local revolt against the newly established regime. He hastened back to Tokyo, taking Katsu's son with him, but on meeting Katsu was amazed to find that the latter was furious with them. Katsu told them to reflect on why they had been in America. According to him it was not for the sake of the Shogunate government or of Katsu himself or of a mere clan; these were all minor considerations in comparison with the future of the nation at large. It was the nation that counted. Katsu gave them the fare and sent them back to America immediately.

When Katsu's son succeded in entering the Naval Academy in 1870, Tomita became a student at Dr Whitney's college as already mentioned. But why a commercial college? Regrettably there is no evidence available to answer this question. However, a likely explanation is that it was Katsu's intention to groom capable persons who would contribute to the modernization of Japan to the point where it could compete with Western countries. It was in this way that Tomita came to know Whitney and later recommended him to Mori as the most suitable person to teach at the school that Mori was determined to establish in Tokyo.[13]

Against this background it would seem quite natural that Tomita, when he later met the die-hard American protectionist H. C. Carey in 1875, promised Carey that he would translate his *Principles of Social Science* (1858–9) into Japanese in order to offer it to his compatriots. As it turned out, he was too busy to carry out the task himself and the Japanese version was prepared by a friend of his, Inukai Tsuyoshi, a graduate from Fukuzawa's school.[14] However, in the preface to the fourth edition of the book, Tomita stated that Carey had told him to be wary about what the Westerners had done and were still doing to the Asiatic nations. It would seem equally natural that Tomita also wrote a preface to the Japanese translation of the protectionists' bible, *Das nationale System der politischen Oekonomie* (1841) by Friedrich List, in which he stressed that Japan ought not to follow the way proposed so authoritatively by Adam Smith and his disciples.

The second illustration of the importance of nationalism arises from a rather mysterious change in Mori's attitude towards Whitney. Before the arrival of the Whitneys, Mori wrote to his friend, the then vice-Consul at San Francisco, Takagi Saburo, that he intended to start a business school as soon as Whitney arrived. But soon after the Whitneys reached Japan in August 1875, Mori wrote in a letter to Takagi that he was greatly disappointed in Whitney's person and calibre. Other people concerned, such as the trustees Fukuzawa and Mitsukuri, received Whitney warmly but, strangely enough, Mori suddenly appeared to have lost his enthusiasm for a business school.[15]

It was only by means of the persistent persuasion of other supporters such as Fukuzawa and the offer from Katsu of a substantial sum of money (1,000 yen at the contemporary value) that Mori was finally induced to open the school.[16] (It is interesting, incidentally, that Katsu and Fukuzawa, notorious for their animosity towards each other, co-operated – though probably unaware of it – in the launching of the business school.)

The reason for Mori's disappointment and loss of enthusiasm is not known. No evidence is available but a clue might lie in a document, most probably written by Mori himself, entitled 'Why is a commercial school needed?' In this it is stated that Japan is geographically situated more favourably than any other Asian country and that, if the talent of its people were to be properly cultivated, Japan would not fail to surpass all of the nations of the world.[17] Thus, it is likely that Mori's disappointment in Whitney could have arisen from the difference in their ideas which quickly became apparent. For Mori, the school should be for the training of future businesspeople who could compete with, and protect their country's interest from, overseas merchants; Whitney, on the other hand, must have believed in the necessity of business education in the technical sense of the term, just as he had been engaged in at his own college in Newark.

If such was the case, we may safely conclude that Mori's disappointment in Whitney, Katsu's fury with Tomita, and the spirit in which Fukuzawa wrote the prospectus all derived from the same source, namely nationalism or, more properly, nationalism and enlightenment rolled into one. This was the ideal foundation of the first business school and the spirit that characterized the economic thought of Fukuzawa and his friends. Needless to say, Enlightenment in its original or genuine form had little to do with nationalism. On the contrary, what mattered in the Enlightenment in France, Germany, England or Scotland, for example, was not a particular nation but humanity in general or human reason with which to perceive the law of nature as they used to call it. Enlightenment in its later versions, i.e. enlightenment in late-starting countries, seems more often than not to have been coloured by nationalism.

What, in the circumstances, therefore, were the subjects actually taught at the earliest stage of the school's existence? Regrettably, again, hardly anything is left in the way of evidence. There is only a simplified version of rules and regulations of the evening course at the school, according to which lectures were to be delivered from seven o'clock to nine o'clock every evening except for Saturdays and Sundays. Subjects to be taught were the Japanese translation by Fukuzawa of *Bryant and Stratton's Common School Bookkeeping*, English conversation, grammar and penmanship, mathematics and geography.[18] It may safely be presumed that the same subjects at least, and probably more, were taught in the regular day course.

Another document, dated August 1876 and entitled 'The Simplified Regulations of the Commercial Training School',[19] reveals that the whole course extended over eighteen months, divided into three terms. The subjects to be taught were, in the first term, mainly English and, in the second and third terms, mostly practical or technical matters such as promissory notes, deed-writing, catalogue-making, invoices, bank bills and bills of exchange.

Meanwhile, just two months after the launching of the school, Mori was appointed Ambassador to Peking. His request to the Tokyo Council that it should take over the school was accepted. Then, in September of the following year, responsibility for the school was once again transferred, this time from the Council to the Tokyo Prefectural Government, thus completing the transition from a private to a public institution. In 1878 the Prefectural Government decided that it could no longer afford to pay the high salary that Whitney received and so discharged him, though the contract between him and his former employer Mori or rather the Tokyo Council had not yet expired. Two American teachers of commercial subjects were employed in his place.

Three years after the 'Simplified Regulations', more formalized regulations were drawn up. The school now offered students, aged at least fifteen, a two-year course in four terms. The first and second terms were devoted to theory, the third to theory and practice, and the fourth to practice only. In the following year, 1880, the school again changed its regulations, extending the whole course to three years composed of six terms. In 1881, the regulations were changed once more, moving from a three-year to a five-year course. Thus, step by step, the school was coming closer to being a more systematic institution. Those five years were divided into ten terms; the subjects to be taught in each term were by and large the same in nature, i.e. mostly practical, but subjects of a more theoretical kind, such as international treaties, commercial law (national and foreign) and world history, were also introduced in the fifth and sixth terms. Political economy was also included. In addition to 'Fawcett's short political economy', and F. A. Walker's *Science of Wealth* (1871), which were already listed in the 1880 regulations, one more book, A. L. Perry's *Elements of Political Economy* (1865) is now listed as though to ascertain the nature of the subject. It is not certain whether 'Fawcett's short political economy' means the *Manual of Political Economy* (1863) by Henry Fawcett or *Political Economy for Beginners* (1870) by his wife, M. G. Fawcett, but, together with the other two books in the ninth and tenth terms, there can be no doubt that the political economy that was taught in the Commercial Training School was nothing but the popularized version of classical political economy, despite the nationalist spirit that lay at the basis of the school.[20] The English-language textbooks were lent to the students, following the practice in Fukuzawa's school and in some others, thus blazing the trail for university libraries to come.

The number of students increased steadily; in 1881, enrolment was as high as 200. But at that point the school encountered a crisis when the Prefectural Government decided that it could no longer support the school and planned to close it after the end of the financial year, i.e. July 1881. The then Minister of Education reminded the Governor of Tokyo Prefecture how useful and beneficial the school had proved so far. A substantial sum of financial aid was offered by the Ministry of Agriculture and Trade. Three years later, in March 1884, the school was transferred to that Ministry, thus becoming a national institution, and was renamed Tokyo Commercial School. Most of its graduates went into the business world.

It is worth adding a note about the further development of the school. What had originated as Mori's private school developed, in 1887, into a well-organized higher educational institution entitled the Higher Commercial School, which was renamed the Tokyo Higher Commercial School in 1902. This was in order to distinguish it from sister schools set up in Kobe and Osaka about the turn of the century as successors to the Kobe and Osaka Commercial Schools respectively, which were launched a few years after their forerunner in Tokyo. Although the Tokyo Higher Commercial School was not yet fully of university standard, it was certainly approaching it because as early as 1897 the school instituted a one-year, and then in the following year a two-year, postgraduate course, when it was authorized to give those who completed the course the degree of BA Commerce. It was not until 1920 that the school officially took the name of university, calling itself the Tokyo University of Commerce, but it had substantially attained that status already.

If this story is to be set in an international context, it may be recalled that the first Handelshochschule (College of Commerce) in Leipzig was set up as late as 1898; that the first colleges for the exclusive study of commerce were set up in Chicago and California only in 1898, though more than ten similar institutions were immediately to follow until the well-known Harvard Business School was opened in 1908; that the London School of Economics and Political Science, with l'Ecole Livre des Sciences Politiques in Paris as its prototype, was started by Sydney Webb and some others for 'training in administration, whether commercial or governmental', in 1895;[21] and that the first faculty of commerce in an English university was instituted in Birmingham in 1902 with the economic historian Sir William James Ashley as its first professor.[22] From these dates it may be seen that the time-lag between the more advanced countries and the late-starter Japan is unexpectedly small in the field of business education.

6

THE BIRTH OF A LIMITED COMPANY

The aim of this chapter is to describe the events surrounding the launching of the first incorporated or joint stock company in Japan, or perhaps one might say the first limited company in Japan, which took place in 1869, only a year after the Meiji Restoration. In those days there was of course no commercial law or even civil law in Japan, so that in the strictly legal sense it was not a limited company, but for all practical purposes it was something of the kind.

The company in question is called Maruzen, or Maruya as it was first known. Situated in Nihonbashi, one of the oldest, busiest and most fashionable parts of Tokyo, it has long been noted, particularly by intellectuals and by the Westerners living in Japan, for its trade in Western books and stationery. For quite some time it was almost the only window, as it were, through which to see Western culture but naturally, with the arrival of a number of competitors, that is no longer the case. Most scholars and writers, such as Natsume Soseki or Akutagawa Ryunosuke, were customers. It is said that Natsume's wife used to complain that he often spent more in Maruzen than he received by way of salary. One of Natsume's three earliest literary pieces (January 1905) was published in Maruzen's monthly magazine *Gakuto*. Hagiwara Sakutaro, in his famous poem (February 1917), declared: 'How I wish I had visited France, but, alas, France is so very far away.' Without Maruzen such a poem would not have come about. Kajii Motojiro, in his well-known short story (January 1925), imagined a lemon he happened to have with him to be a tiny bomb, which he secretly placed on a gorgeous book on fine arts in one of the shelves of Maruzen. In his imgination it exploded after he had left the shop and destroyed everything there.

Such was the reputation of Maruzen, which, despite being surpassed in latter years by late-starting firms such as Mitsui, Mitsubishi and Sumitomo, remains the oldest incorporated company in Japan. Our concern here is to examine how it came to be launched well over a century ago and how the spirit of the age influenced that launching.

The story starts with a medical practitioner called Hayashi Yuteki. Unfortunately, all of the personal documents related to the first half of his life and to the earliest days of the company were lost as a result of the great fire in the Nihonbashi area in 1876. According to less authentic literature, which was compiled much later mainly on the basis of the memories of a younger cousin of his who worked for the company, Hayashi, after seven years of medical practice in Edo, gave it up in order to enter Fukuzawa Yukichi's private school (the forerunner, as said before, of Keio University). The record of his registration at the school in 1867 is still kept in Keio University. The reason why he did this is unknown, but very probably it was because of the deep respect that he must have had for Fukuzawa, although the latter was only two years older than himself.

What is strange, however, is that Hayashi, though he may indeed have stopped being a medical practitioner for a while, did not entirely leave the profession. In Yokohama, and not in Edo where Fukuzawa's school was, he rented a room from which he went, perhaps daily, to work as the director of a newly established syphilis hospital. How it was possible for a student of Fukuzawa's to be engaged in medical work in Yokohama in those days, when the very first railway in Japan between the two cities as yet belonged to the future, remains a mystery. Furthermore, he vacated the room in the following year and rented a small house, still in Yokohama. There, with three friends, he opened a shop for second-hand Japanese books under the name of Maruya. Thus, although, as we shall see later, the official starting date of Maruya is given in the prospectus of Maruya and Co. as 1869, the actual beginning was then and there. Hayashi then moved again to yet another part of Yokohama, where he opened two adjacent shops one selling Western books which were perhaps new and not second-hand, the other selling medicines. In addition, he seems to have resumed medical practice. As evidence of this, Fukuzawa says in a letter to a friend, which is dated March 1870, that he had recently suffered from an infectious disease and had received medical care from some distinguished doctors, Western as well as Japanese, one of whom was Hayashi. Once again, how Hayashi's studentship was compatible with all of these activities is a puzzle. *Maruzen Hyakunen-shi* (A Hundred Years of Maruzen and Co.) similarly connects Hayashi's business with his teacher Fukuzawa but gives no reference.[1]

It says that Fukuzawa trusted Hayashi with the importation of Western goods, a task which he had long been anxious to do himself, and that it was none other than Fukuzawa who discovered in Hyashi the qualities and talents of a businessman. This may well have been the case but it is not endorsed by evidence.

On Fukuzawa's part, there is nothing to suggest or to prove his involvement in the launching of Maruya and Co. There is no mention of it in his famous and fascinating *Fukuo Jiden* (Fukuzawa's Autobiography) or anywhere in his huge number of letters. But his interest in the business is fairly clear, especially in some of his letters written between 1870 and 1873. For instance, he asked in a letter to Hayashi how he was getting on with his business, and in a letter to a friend suggested that the friend place an order with Maruya. Furthermore, he even tried to persuade a disciple of his to become a full-time member of the company.[2]

Maruya and Co., having started in such a way, seems to have proceeded smoothly. In 1874, five years after publication of the prospectus, a book entitled *Tokyo Shinhanjoki* (New Tokyo in Prosperity), which was written in Chinese style by a contemporary journalist, Hattori Busho, following the example of another book in Chinese style published years previously, by Terakado Seiken, under the title *Edo Hanjoki* (Edo in Prosperity), referred to Maruya as a Western bookshop:

> An unheard-of grandeur in a bookshop. English, French, German and other books come in month after month, day after day. All of the wall is covered with shelves, which have transparent glass doors, and all of the shelves are filled with leather-bound books, red or black. Their golden titles shine and glitter.[3]

An illustrated book, which shows a view of the Nihonbashi area completely reconstructed after the fire, depicts Maruya.[4] The ground floor sold Japanese books and stationery, and the first floor Western books. The shop next door sold sundry imported goods. Other, separate shops sold medicines, furniture, and Western clothes. All of these shops belonged to the company. In addition, as a financial centre for them all, there was a bank called Maruya Ginko (Maruya Bank).

Maruya had in the meantime been nicknamed Maruzen by Hayashi and his friends. The chairman was officially registered not under his real name of Hayashi Yuteki but under the fictitious name of Maruya

Zenpachi; hence *Maru*ya *Zen*pachi, a common way of nicknaming by way of abbreviation. Maruzen, the nickname, came to be registered as the official name of the company.

The boom days of Maruzen lasted until the deflationary policy of the Minister of Finance, Matsukata Masayoshi, affected the group badly. The Maruya Bank, in spite of Hayashi's best efforts, went bankrupt and a trading company, Boeki Shokai, which he had established separately from Maruya, followed suit.

However, let us return to the starting point of the company. When looking at the prospectus, *Maruya Shosha no Ki*, dated January 1869,[5] it is difficult not to be struck by the strength of the public spirit in which this private company was about to be launched. The text begins: 'In order to do something, whatever it may be, one ought to consider one's own rank and position. When I think about the position in which I am placed now . . .' The identity of 'I' is undoubtedly Hayashi himself, although the identity of the actual writer is less certain. Hayashi's nephew, Hayashi Torakichi, who also worked for Maruzen, is said to have recollected that it was most unlikely for his uncle to have written it himself, since he had been far too busy to do so.[6] We shall return to this question later. The writer, whoever it might have been, continues: 'When I think about the position in which I am placed now, I must say that I am neither a person who occupies an official post in the government nor am I a person who is privately employed by someone else. I am a free person.' But instead of proceeding to say that he is therefore an independent individual who may do what he likes, he says: 'I am a Japanese who can do what he can and what he must.' Thus, the intended meaning is not an individual as such but a Japanese or a member of that nation. As a free Japanese he believed it to be a self-evident duty to contribute to the prosperity of his country and to the happiness of his compatriots. The passages that follow are very much in accordance with this opening statement.

On the other hand, rather like an intellectual who lived in the age of 'civilization and culture' (Bunmei Kaika), the writer claims that it is vanity to regard his country as a sacred land surpassing all other nations of the world or as a self-contained country sufficiently provided with all of the necessities of life. To the younger generation in Japan today such a notion as sacred land or self-contained country must surely sound nonsensical, but to the older generation this enlightened consciousness will by no means appear old-fashioned when they recall their memories of pre-war or inter-war times when they were taught that Japan was a god-made, holy country never impinged upon by any foreign nation whatsoever for thousands of years.

According to the writer, there is nothing more obvious than the difference in the degree of civilization that lies between Japan and the Western countries. That difference originates in the inherited cancer insidiously spreading as a result of the age-long policy of isolationism. Thus, the immediate priority must be to cut away this cancer, and thereby enter the sphere of civilization, in order to cope with the Westerners. While there are, indeed, many things to be done in that regard, such as matters relating to all sorts of learning, to the army and navy, and to industry and the arts, the most important of all is trade. The reason is evident. The true incentive for foreigners to come to Japan lies not in amity but in trade. Although there are foreigners who are in Japan to teach various kinds of learning and industrial techniques or to lecture in modern law or to instruct in the military arts, from the viewpoint of actual international relations they are an exceptional minority. The principal aim of foreigners is to make a profit by means of trade.

The writer continues, combining his argument with the above-mentioned national mission as he sees it: 'It would be contrary to my duty as a Japanese if I stood idly by while foreigners kept the right of business and trade in this country in their own hands.' He is convinced that if the Japanese people become employees in foreign merchants' companies or invite foreigners into Japanese companies to ask for their advice, they will lose their autonomy and the name of being an independent nation. He goes on to say:

> With independence once lost, neither learnings nor arts and techniques would be of any use. Thus, leaving those studies to other scholars and politics to those who are in government offices, I for one, as a free Japanese, consider it to be my duty to engage myself in trade and to make the business of Japan stand on an independent footing, thereby endeavouring to ensure that my compatriots keep their peace of mind.

As to the nature of the proposed business, the writer says:

> Among the essentials for human life, the most important of all are education and medical treatments. However, Western books, as the indispensable means for the former, and medicine and medical instruments as the indispensable means for the

> latter, are in desperately short supply. Therefore our company will first of all specialize in the buying and selling of these commodities.

It must have been quite natural for Hayashi, as a medical practitioner, to give priority to medicine and medical instruments. Nevertheless, the spirit that permeates the prospectus *Maruya Shosha no Ki* is clear enough. On the one hand, it was an understanding of international realities, an understanding which might well be regarded as excellent compared with the standard of the time, which sought to deny the unfounded traditional belief in the holiness and wealth or self-sufficiency of Japan. In other words, it was Enlightenment based on realism. On the other hand, it was a duty-consciousness or nationalism which urged him not to sit back and do nothing against the trade monopoly of overseas merchants. Here, too, is an example of enlightenment and nationalism combined into one; a characteristic, as we have seen, of the intellectuals in late-starting countries such as Japan. To repeat the observations of earlier chapters, the distinction is clear between the notable thinkers of the eighteenth-century European Enlightenment and those of its Japanese counterpart a century later. What mattered, for example, to the French thinkers of the time such as Helvetius, Diderot, Rousseau, Quesnay and many others was the human nature with which to perceive natural order in the widest sense of the term. When Immanuel Kant wrote his *Kritik der reinen Vernunft*, it was the pure (*reine*) reason that he was always seeking. When, likewise, Adam Smith said that all human beings are by nature interest-bound, it could be anybody regardless of nationality that he had in mind.

The concluding part of the prospectus is as interesting as its opening part. It says:

> People are destined either to flourish or to perish. The difference comes from whether they follow the right path or the wrong path. If one person decides everything on his own, he cannot expect to be corrected if he errs. If some people combine themselves into a company, they could be expected to follow reason by correcting each other's mistakes. And that is why we associate ourselves, some investing their money, and others their own persons, thereby launching a company under the name of Maruya.

Those who offered money were named 'Motokin Shachu' or stock-offering members while the others were 'Hataraki Shachu' or labour-offering members. Although it was a clumsy description, there is no doubt that this was a step forward, a great step forward, towards the modern idea of a limited company, as has been suggested above. Hataraki Shachu, or labour-offering members, were not just clerks but full-time members, whereas Motokin Shachu or stock-offering members were simply shareholders. 'Clerk' was described variously as employee or servant. Fukuzawa, in the above-mentioned letter to a disciple of his, advised the man to join the company as a full-time member by offering not only stock but labour. He told the man that he, Fukuzawa, had become a member, meaning a shareholder. (Incidentally, Fukuzawa also became the biggest shareholder when Hayashi established a law consultancy named Jiriki Shakai, meaning self-help firm, in 1877 and the Maruya Bank in 1879.) The Motokin Shachu were no doubt members of limited liability, whereas the Hataraki Shachu could be members of either unlimited or limited liability; nothing is explicitly defined, however. On the other hand, if we look at the rules and regulations of the Maruya Bank and the Boeki Shokai (or Trading Company, already referred to above), it is amazing to find that they are already almost a limited company as such. Here again we see how fast modernization proceeded. Even with all of the clumsiness and vagueness in phraseology, the rules of Maruya and Co. contain some interesting clauses relating not only to the members but also to some other points including, for instance, what might be called inner-company democracy.

One outstanding matter still to be dealt with is the identity of the writer of the prospectus *Maruya Shosha no Ki*. As said above, there is no direct evidence but there is indirect or circumstancial evidence. *Maruzen Hyakunenshi* (A Hundred Years of Maruzen and Co.), which was published in three volumes some years ago, states without giving any reference that the writer might have been one of the four original full-time members, a man called Sawai Hidezo,[7] but this does not seem very convincing. On the other hand, what has just been described above as 'circumstancial evidence' comes down in favour of Fukuzawa as the author.[8] First, the style in which the prospectus is written is very like Fukuzawa's. Second, between the text, or what may rather be called a preamble, and the regulations themselves, the writer inserts in a somewhat incidental way a chapter from Fukuzawa's *Domo Oshiegusa* (A Reader for the Infant), which was in fact a summarized translation of Benjamin Franklin's autobiography encouraging diligence and frugality. Third, and more significant still, within the text there is a reference both to a commercial school and to bookkeeping. The writer says that he is completely inexperienced in, and ignorant of, anything relating to business and that, since there is currently no commercial school anywhere in Japan or anybody to teach bookkeeping, he is determined to regard his company as a sort of commercial school in order to become acquainted with business and trade. This cannot fail to remind us of the bookkeeping textbook *Choai no Ho* (A Guide to Bookkeeping) which Fukuzawa came to publish four years later in 1873 and which was a translation of Bryant and Stratton's *Common School Bookkeeping*, published in New York only two years previously, and also of 'Shogakko o tatsuru no Shui', the prospectus of the very first commercial school in Japan, which it is clear that he wrote in 1875 on behalf of the two other trustees and himself. As noted in Chapter 5, in the translator's preface to the former Fukuzawa describes bookkeeping as an example of real learning as opposed to vain learning and expresses the wish that study of it may contribute something to the reformation of the economy of the nation at large and thereby to an increase in national power. In the latter, as has also been made clear already, he writes that the difference in wealth and skill among the Japanese merchants used to be no more than a private matter but that it was now a public duty for merchants to compete with foreigners in business and trade. Does this not resemble Maruya's prospectus not only in tone but also in the argument itself which advocated the duty to strive to do away with the monopoly of the overseas merchants and thereby to contribute to the prosperity of the whole nation?

It might seem strange to some people that Fukuzawa, that all-round champion of the Japanese Enlightenment, had such a trait of nationalism in his thought. Those who treat Fukuzawa as a liberal in economic thought as well as in political thought are used to referring the reader to his early writings such as 'Tojin Orai' (Foreigners In and Out) and *Seiyo Jijo, Gaihen* (Conditions in the West, vol. 2). The former, though kept unpublished and only printed many years later, is his very first work, written some years before the Restoration. If read carefully, it is clear that all that he wanted there was to persuade the ordinary reader that the long-held policy of isolationism was detrimental to the development of the country. Free trade or protectionism was not, and could not have been, an issue yet. And the latter work is, as already noted, not his own writing but simply a translation of part of a textbook for beginners by a Scottish publisher, namely *Chambers's Educational Course: Political Economy, for Use in Schools, and for Private Instruction.*[9] The original text is composed of two parts, the first of which Fukuzawa translated, leaving the second untouched. The first part has hardly anything to do with economics proper, far less with freedom or protection, so it is quite unjustified to talk about free trade and *laissez-faire* in Fukuzawa's thought on the basis of such writing.

In the early days of the Meiji era there were already heated discussions about the problem of free trade or protection. *Meiroku Zasshi* (Meiji Six Journal), the journal of Meirokusha (Meiji Six Society), an association organized by Mori and his friends in the sixth year of the Meiji era (1873) for the explicit purpose of enlightenment, was one of the arenas for debate. Within its pages some argued for and others against free trade, and Fukuzawa was among the latter, as we have already seen. But, more especially, in his own periodical *Minkan Zasshi* (Popular Magazine), he declared that foreigners came to Japan not to do its people a favour by imparting to them knowledge and virtue and thereby leading them to civilization but, on the contrary, simply to make a profit on trade. Does this point not closely resemble not only the argument itself but the phraseology used in the relevant passage in Maruya's prospectus? Thus, it may safely be concluded that the prospectus of the first limited company in Japan was written by none other than Fukuzawa himself, in whose thought enlightenment and nationalism were, once again, inseparably fused.[10]

7

THE BIRTH OF ECONOMIC JOURNALISM

If Nishi, Tsuda, Kanda, Fukuzawa and some others were the economic liberals of the first generation, Taguchi Ukichi may be said to be of the second generation. Indeed, when Nishi was appointed as the principal of the Military Academy that was newly established at Numazu in 1868, Taguchi was one of the students.[1] It is not clear how Taguchi became a convinced subscriber to economic liberalism at the beginning of his career as an economic writer but he held to the belief to the end. His first book was *Jiyu Koeki Nihon Keizairon* (On Free Trade Japanese Economy, 1878) written at the age of only twenty-four.

In this he writes that, since a self-sufficient economy does not necessarily bring about the desired satisfaction for humans, division of labour is the natural outcome. Division of labour brings about a natural diversity of trades, which is secured by free exchange between individuals and, likewise, between nations. Some people assert that, since there is still a large number of ex-*samurai* who are unemployed (a natural consequence of long-lived feudalism), there should be a policy to develop some government-sponsored firms, with attractive conditions, to induce them to work there. But this is to benefit a small minority at the cost of the large majority; the one gains what the other loses, so that the sum total does not increase but remains the same. The best way to ensure that the nation benefits as much as possible is simply to leave everything well alone. When left free to choose, every person will go where the greatest gain is expected; will select a profession which fits him or her most and which brings the greatest returns.[2] If, therefore, the freedom of choice of profession and the freedom of exchange within the nation is the most beneficial to the nation, then the freedom of trade between nations is only an application of that truth in a wider context.

Feudal society has its own customs and commodities. For example, it is natural in feudalism for *samurai* to have swords at their waists. But once feudalism is abolished, then *samurai* and their swords become outdated. 'To try to keep remnants of feudalism now resembles an attempt to throw birds into the water or to throw fish into the sky.' Privilege and protection belong to the past. They have been taken over by freedom and competition.[3]

> Why do we spare no labour and work as hard as we can? Is it not for the sake of earning money? Would one exert oneself for someone else if one had no right to one's rewards? The government, too, has no right to transfer the revenue of our own making to somebody else. If the government were ever to do so, it would do so only by invading our proper right. Protective duties are nothing but the means to increase someone's interest by decreasing someone else's interest, and that is why they are not within the government's right.[4]

The same principle applies to international trade. Suppose it costs ten yen to produce a roll of woollen cloth in Japan and only seven yen in a Western country. In such a case the government might, for instance, levy customs duties of five yen on the imported cloth because the free importation of Western cloth will cause a loss to the Japanese cloth-makers. The price of the imported cloth would not sell at less than twelve yen, whereas Japanese makers could sell at eleven yen and so gain one yen per roll. However, 'those who buy cloth are obliged to lose three yen per roll compared with when there were no protective duties.' Thus, 'the more trades rely on protective duties, the greater is the loss to the nation as a whole.'[5]

It was this firm belief that later inspired Taguchi to start the first economic periodical in 1879 in order to discuss economic issues and, by so doing, to popularize the *laissez-faire* principle. In the preface to the first number he describes the background to the launch and his motives. When he was an official in the Ministry of Finance, he came to know the so-called 'employee foreigner' A. A. Shand,[6] adviser to the Ministry on the establishing of national banks, which was then under discussion at the suggestion of Shibusawa Eiichi. One day Taguchi, looking at *The Economist* lying on Shand's desk, told Shand that he believed that Japan should also have that kind of periodical. To this Shand replied that probably Japan was not yet rich enough to have one. 'Although it was no more than a passing remark in coversation, it left a very great impression on me. I promised him that

I would some day launch an economic periodical of this kind and would show it to him.' Thereafter, owing to his work as a government official and also to his writing of a book, which was to be published under the title *Jiyu Koeki Nihon Keizairon* (On Free Trade Japanese Economy), he had been unable to find enough time to edit a periodical. However, when Shibusawa, who had already been successful in establishing a national bank, proposed to Taguchi that he should amalgamate two small magazines of his, one a banking and the other a finance magazine, in order to start a more general and more regular economic periodical, Taguchi was only too willing to accept the offer and was very grateful for it. The result was *Tokyo Keizai Zasshi*, with the explicit English title *The Tokyo Economist* alongside the Japanese one. Taguchi concludes the preface by saying that the periodical must be impartial and must deal with economic matters at large, without being confined to banking or finance. He urges readers, if they are patriotically minded at all, to subscribe to his periodical and by so doing demonstrate to the world that Japan is now rich enough to start an economic periodical.[7]

Nineteen months after the launching of *Tokyo Keizai Zasshi* or *The Tokyo Economist*, a rival economic periodical was started in August 1880 under the title of *Tokai Keizai Shinpo* (Tokai New Economic Review). Just as the former announced in its first number that it would contain articles and reviews on matters related to banking, commerce and finance in order to inform people of the economic situation at home and abroad, so the latter announced in its first issue that it would comprise articles, reviews and statisics concerning both the domestic and foreign economies, and would thereby serve the needs of those who were engaged in business.

From such announcements it would seem that there was little difference between them. However, their opposing viewpoints were immediately apparent, because the very first editorial in *Tokai Keizai Shinpo* says:

> The National economy is not the same as a cosmopolite economy, nor is it the same as a private economy. What constitutes a mass, lying between the individual and humanity at large, and separate from other masses, is the state. Each state has its own race, language, custom, law and civilization. That is why their interests are nothing less than various, and so are their economies. If it is not possible to combine all countries of the world in one single community without different interests and

> without conflict and strife for evermore, it is equally impossible to establish an economy which is universally applicable. Nowadays there is an increasing number of scholars who debate economic problems but the number of those who write books or issue periodicals on economic subjects is very small. And that small number is limited to those who argue on the vain principle of cosmopolitism. That is why we are now launching this periodical, *Tokai Keizai Shinpo*.

The writer goes on to say that 'protective duties are indispensable for a country with scarcely any manufactures'. Without them industry cannot grow and trade can barely prosper. Only agriculture will endure. Some people denounce protectionism and claim that all matters relating to humanity can best be served by leaving everything to nature. By so doing, despite some temporary inconveniences that might follow, everything will eventually come right without fail. If the government chooses to intervene to remove such temporary inconveniences, without waiting for nature to put them right, then many evils are inevitable. This is the so-called *laissez-faire* theory. But *laissez-faire* applies only to the government's improper intervention in the past, such as setting prices and wages, permitting monopolies, prohibiting workers' unions, forbidding a free press, and so on. However, all of these actions constitute improper behaviour by government at any time.

> What we want is to let the government do its proper, and not improper, duty. What, then, is its proper duty? It is no more than to protect its own people's safety and welfare from invasion by other countries. Is it not invasion when they overwhelm our industry and shrink our trade, thereby impoverishing and weakening us? If so, then it is the proper duty of our government to protect its people from them.[8]

Tokyo Keizai Zasshi answered immediately but only briefly. 'Having heard for some time of a periodical by the name of *Tokai Keizai Shinpo* being planned in opposition to us, we have been waiting for it to appear.' However, the editorial is not impressed. As far as the first issue is concerned, it comments, the reasoning is so vague that it is hard to discern why it argues for protective trade. It talks of the importation of commodities produced in advanced and civilized countries and seems to imply that those commodities suppress Japan's commodities or rather the industries that produce them. But any industry which is so susceptible is least advantageous to Japan. Why, then, should money be spent to protect the very industry that is disadvantageous? If the protectionists are worried about the outflow of money in payment of such imported commodities, then they are simply wrong, because the commodities for which there is demand are bought with superfluous money. Nothing could be more advantageous to Japan.

> The reality of trade consists in the fact that exports regulate imports and imports regulate exports. What they [the protectionists] aim at is only to increase exports and to decrease imports. This means that they do not know anything about the reality of trade.[9]

Besides this editorial, *Tokyo Keizai Zasshi* included a signed article by Nagasaka Ikichi, the substance of which is by and large the same. The writer comments that *Tokai Keizai Shinpo* asks how Japan can expect to be strong and wealthy if she is merely engaged in agriculture and totally depends on other countries' industry and trade. This theory, he says, sounds true but is in fact false. When a country's industry, trade and transport have not yet been fully developed, all commodities manufactured there cannot help being more expensive than, and inferior in quality to, those imported from abroad. 'Nothing is more harmful than for a government to intervene in people's trade and to levy duties on good and cheap imports in order to increase demand for poor and expensive commodities produced within the country.' Can it be justified to protect a small number of traders at the expense of a large number of consumers? 'Protective duties are the means to make goods scarce and free trade is the means to make them abundant.'[10]

Tokai Keizai Shinpo immediately responded with a signed article by Kato Taiki. According to this, the commodities that are adversely affected by foreign commodities are not those which are unsuited to the natural conditions of the country and consequently cannot be of benefit even if produced through hard effort but are those which, once developed, will be of great benefit but which, for the moment, are left undeveloped because of the lack of skilled labour and improved machinery. It is the intention of protectionists to prevent foreign goods from coming in and to promote the skill of artisans over a period of some years, so that manufactured commodities in Japan will in that time become cheaper than those which are currently imported. It will therefore be much wiser to bear temporary inconveniences in order to attain lasting benefit. Moreover, in time of possible war, the importation of foreign commodities will stop, by which point it will be too late for Japan suddenly to try to start producing those commodities with such a shortage of skill and machinery.[11]

Meanwhile *Tokyo Keizai Zasshi* printed an editorial which referred to the protectionist Henry Charles Carey:

> There was a Mr Henry Carey in America who, fearing the centralized power of London to absorb all of the commerce of the world, argued for the protection of America. His argument became one of the fortresses for the protectionists to maintain their mistaken views.

The editorial then pointed out that, if one feared London's centralization, one should pursue free trade because protective laws and regulated commerce would serve only to drive away commodities to London and thereby add to London's centralization. London was for European and American countries what Hong Kong was for Asian countries. Protection could result only in making Hong Kong even more of a central market.[12]

Tokyo Keizai Zasshi carried another article signed by Nagasaka which aimed to contradict Kato's article in *Tokai Keizai Shinpo*. Nagasaka maintained that the question of whether a trade grew or not depended on whether it was of a suitable kind. A suitable one grew with no need of protection, whereas an unsuitable one could not grow even with all manner of protection. He took as an example the manufacture of shoes, umbrellas and soap. Without any protection these had been competing in the market with foreign makes and eventually had beaten the competition. Any industry which could grow without protection proved that it was not suitable for Japan. Kato was also wrong in his reference to a possible case of war. When America started the war against Britain, it at once found alternative markets and, in spite of the stoppage of imports from Britain, won the war.

The same issue of *Tokyo Keizai Zasshi* contained another article, signed by a Matsumura Kozaburo, which said:

> Is it not human nature to strive for greater reward? There is no reason why one should use one's capital and labour to produce commodities which are unprofitable. Do those products which are profitable, such as raw silk or tea, not steadily increase?

> Unprofitable industries can last for only a very few years, even if they are placed under protection. The writer in *Tokai Keizai Shinpo* refrains from stating which industry is to be protected and what length of time would be necessary for it to grow sufficiently independent.

He concludes by saying that it is only because one country is favoured by having some products and another by having others that there is any foreign trade in the world at all. If a country chooses not to import other countries' commodities, in case of a possible war, then that country must produce every kind of commodity within its own borders and at the same cost as in any other country, which is an absurd supposition. Every country is at one and the same time a producer and a consumer or, in other words, an exporter and an importer.[13]

Tokai Keizai Shinpo at once printed an article by one Yamato Gotaro, a pen-name meaning 'defender of Japan', to contradict these two articles. Japan, he argues, is mild in its climate and fertile in its soil, so that it produces plenty of materials which can be manufactured. Therefore, a protective policy will lead to a growth in industry and to an increase in the skill of workers. If the scale of production grows to a sufficient extent, then the commodities produced will rival or even excel those imported without any need of further protection. How can it be said that industry which is presently underdeveloped is not fitted for this country? Nagasaka uses shoes, umbrellas and soap as examples of industrial commodities which have developed without protective duties but these are not relevant to his argument. The shoe-maker to whom he refers has borrowed a large sum of money from the government authorities, at little or no interest, and has received an order for some tens of thousands of pairs of shoes from the army. This is nothing but indirect protection, or direct protection if customs duties are taken into account. Umbrellas are simple to make, need little in the way of capital or machinery, and use silk, which is a domestic product, as their main material. Much the same applies to soap-making. Therefore, these products cannot be used to endorse his argument for free trade. Matsumura's criticism is more or less to the same effect. He accuses protectionists of not stating what kinds of commmodity are to be protected and for how long. This was not done simply because conditions vary from commodity to commodity. However, it would suffice to quote the example of England: it claims to be the upholder of the principle of free trade but the fact is that its industry has attained its present prosperity only as a result of the protective policy that it previously practised for a long time.[14]

Tokyo Keizai Zasshi replied to this at once in its editorial. Protectionists, it said, maintain that just as the interest of an individual is not the same as that of a nation, so the interest of a nation is not the same as that of the world. Therefore, they claim that free trade will apply only when the borders that divide countries are abolished. But this is wrong. Why is the interest of a nation not in accordance with that of an individual or of the world? A nation is no more than the sum of different individuals and, likewise, the world is the total of different countries. Then again, is the trading between individuals the same as the fighting between them, and the trading between countries the same as the fighting between them? Is it natural that when one side gains, the other side loses? Is it not true that, when a fisherman offers fish and a woodman timber, both parties gain? The interests of agricultural and mining countries are in accord because the former offers rice to the latter and the latter offers gold to the former. Nature's bounty differs from country to country. When some industry in a country cannot make a profit without protection, it simply means that that country is not sufficiently favoured by nature for the good of that industry. If cotton cloth is imported into Japan, farmers gain and weavers lose. Do the protectionists want to favour weavers, through protective duties, by letting farmers lose? Why should cotton-making be protected and rice-growing be suppressed?[15]

To contradict this, *Tokai Keizai Shinpo* used the editorial in the next issue. *Tokyo Keizai Zasshi*, it asserts, does not know that every country has its own particular interest. It does not acknowledge the fact that a protective policy brings forth lasting benefit and increases productive force. It equates a country's being short of skill with a lack of natural assets, and a temporary rise in price with a lasting evil which is caused by protection; this is an entirely wrong interpretation of the matter. Free-traders consider only the inconvenience that the minority suffers, without thinking about the majority's loss. They do not know the significance of self-preservation; through fear of a temporary rise in prices, they tend to depend on the import of all of life's necessities. For a country to rely on other counties for their commodities, without trying to build up its own industry, is nothing less than subjection; independence would be in name only. There are indeed countries, such as Switzerland and Denmark, which are not favoured as regards the fertility of the soil, natural resources, climate, etc. and yet they are trying their best. Japan, in contrast, is favoured with fertile soil, mild climate, and marine and mineral resources. Thus, if Japan is successful in avoiding foreign pressures, it will no doubt become a self-sufficient wealthy country.

There are things which the government should prohibit, such as forged money, gambling and narcotics. There are things which the government should limit, such as some sorts of drugs, explosives and the like. On the other hand, there are things which the government should encourage, such as the building of roads and bridges. These are examples not of so-called government intervention but of its duties. Free-traders wish to abolish all sorts of limitations on business and trade, even customs duties eventually. This is absurd. As foreign trade is closely connected with financial and other national policies, the abolition of foreign trade regulations would necessarily make all domestic policies untenable, because both are so interrelated.[16]

Tokai Keizai Shinpo continues in the same vein in the next number. Since ancient times, it says, those countries such as Portugal, Turkey and India which, despite all of their richness in natural resources, did not regulate foreign trade, were doomed to decay. America and Canada are geographically adjacent, and are similar in many ways, but the former has prospered while the latter has declined; this is only because of the difference in their trade policy, the one exercising protection and the other not. It is claimed that free trade benefits both sides. This may well be so between two nations standing on an equal footing but is not so between two unequal parties. For example, in the trade between Britain and China the former gained enormous profit by selling opium, the detriment of the Chinese people. Likewise, the exchange of gold and silver between Western merchants and the Japanese, which took place after the opening of the Japanese ports to the outer world, resulted in massive profits for the former, who took advantage of the latter's relative ignorance. Even the free-trader Mill advocated a protective policy for those countries which had not yet developed modern industry. This means that he denounced undue intervention by government only in the case of advanced countries such as Britain.[17]

Tokai Keizai Shinpo kept up the argument in the next issue. It pointed out that the trade between agricultural and industrial countries mostly occurs in such a way that the latter either consume or manufacture the products sent to them by the former and that the commodities thus manufactured by the latter go back to the former.

The difference arises simply from the fact that the latter countries, having been engaged in industry since early times, have attained skill which the former countries lack and so can never rival. Free-traders are mistaken in their belief that everything should be left to the natural course of things. It is impossible that the former countries, without protective duties, could ever attain industrial facilities and skill. Furthermore, agricultural countries are liable to famine and so cannot maintain stability. Once they suffer natural disasters, all of their people are bound to suffer, as did the Irish with their potatoes and the Indians with their wheat. The same applies to the Japanese whose main exports are tea and raw silk. The disadvantage under which monocultural countries are placed has already been made clear by H. C. Carey.[18]

Tokyo Keizai Zasshi replied to this only briefly, saying that *Tokai Keizai Shinpo's* reasoning was false. To assert that to buy things from a foreign country is to become its dependent is as absurd as to argue that a newspaper firm, when it buys paper from a paper-making firm, becomes the latter's dependent. The protectionists refer to the free-trader Mill advocating a protective policy for underdeveloped countries, but this is simply Mill's self-contradiction and not that of *Tokyo Keizai Zasshi*.[19] The protectionists seem to suggest that free-traders want to annihilate the border, or even to lead to the ruining of Japan. However:

> Japan is a country which practises free trade and yet it still exists. Britain is also a country which practises free trade. Having been trading with Japan for over twenty years, Britain is still Britain just as Japan is still Japan.

Similarly Tokyo and Osaka have been trading freely with each other for hundreds of years and yet Tokyo is still Tokyo and Osaka is still Osaka. The protectionists seem to believe that all countries which have attained arts and skill can be enriched, regardless of the relative differences in their natural assets. Such a belief is unfounded. If protection were to apply everywhere, it should be profitable to establish manufacturing industry in remote villages or even on the summit of Mt Fuji.[20]

Some signed articles in subsequent issues of *Tokai Keizai Shinpo*, which seek to contradict *Tokyo Keizai Zasshi*, comprise more or less the same arguments. The world is not ruled by one government but is divided into a number of different countries. Thus, it is often the case that a benefit to one country is a loss to another. It is simply because each country has its own soil, climate, and attitudes, and consequently its own interests. For example, Britain adopts free trade as the best policy, whereas America regards protection as the best. It is impractical to assert that free trade applies everywhere. Theory and practice are different from each other. In order to retain independence and to achieve and increase wealth, every country has to improve its agriculture and industry. As for Japan, it is simply because of a shortage of capital and industry that the country has to import so many commodities from foreign countries. The only option remaining for Japan is to levy protective duties on foreign commodities.[21]

No country is the same as any other country with regard to customs, manners, laws, the degree of civilization or anything else, as already mentioned. All that matters in order to retain a country's independence is wealth. In order to increase wealth, agriculture must be improved and industry must be developed. Free-traders say that anything which needs protection does not suit the country and that whatever suits the country develops of itself without protection. To prove that they are mistaken, a simple example may suffice. A young tree, which is the potential timber of the future, will continue to grow unless it experiences hazards such as gales, storms, or heavy snowfalls. Is it a wise policy to leave the tree to suffer until its life is thus destroyed?[22]

Free-traders deliberately refer to protection as being synonymous with wilful interference. It is true that the word interference sounds like something undesirable and harmful in the free world but the truth is that there are two kinds of it, good and bad. The interference that aims to achieve the greatest possible happiness for a nation is not only desirable but also necessary. The difference between good or bad interference arises from whether or not the interference is kept within the bounds of protecting and promoting that happiness. Every country has its government in order to protect the happiness and safety of its people by means of civil and penal laws. This is interference, which varies from country to country according to the difference in customs and in the degree of civilization. Without such interference, leaving everything as it is, the country would be nothing but a barbarous state.[23]

Even England, which is believed to be a champion of freedom in all ways, used to have recourse to protection by accepting artisans who were banished from some Continental countries for religious reasons, by buying various kinds of tools and machines from abroad in order to naturalize and promote industries, by levying heavy duties on imports, by digging canals, and by other similar policies.[24]

It is only in this way that England became wealthy enough to uphold free trade. If it had practised free trade in those days when it was not yet furnished with sufficient skill, machinery and capital, it would no doubt have been impossible to attain its present wealth and prosperity. France prospered when its kings and ministers practised protective policies and declined when they practised free trade regardless of the real situation.

Thus, it is plain whether Japan should follow the example of England or of France. Japan must protect such industries as may suit the country from the invasion of similar foreign industries, and by so doing must try to promote their fast growth and so attain and preserve the prosperity and safety of the country.[25]

Tokyo Keizai Zasshi tries to refute these arguments by carrying a series of signed articles which insist that innovation and protectionism are inconsistent with each other. Innovation, such as the building of railways and canals, is intended to decrease transport expenses and thereby reduce all prices. Protectionists aim to levy taxes on imported foreign commodities and thereby to raise their prices to a level equal to or even higher than those of home commodities. In spite of their claim to promote home industries, high prices are the result all the same. Protectionism and innovation are not compatible. Protectionists claim that protection is not so much an aim as a means; that protection is only a temporary and not a long-term policy; and that protective policies can be abolished when home industries have grown to such an extent as to be able to compete with foreign commodities. They say that a rise in prices may indeed result but that it is only temporary; that the greater benefit of the growth and prosperity of national industries will more than compensate for such a temporary evil. Protectionism, they say, is therefore by no means contradictory to innovation. Such an assumption, however, is not tenable. The power of nature will always prevail. 'Plants in warm countries cannot grow in cold countries. Human power can never compete with natural power.' Just as human talent varies from person to person, so international trade originates in similar natural differences. Its purpose lies in increasing wealth and happiness on both sides through mutual exchange.[26]

Where do the millions come from to offset the rise in prices caused by the heavy taxes on imported goods? The price rises can be defrayed only by cutting the capital bestowed on the industries that fit the nature of the country; in other words, only by everyone reducing consumption of the useful commodities in order to pay for the less useful or useless imports. It is just like poor relief.

> It is obvious from human experience in all parts of the world that if money be spent for the relief of one hundred people today, more money will have to be spent for the relief of two hundred people tomorrow. It is simply because any person, once relieved in this way, becomes accustomed to the lazy way of life. Is it not an illusion to believe that, once the poor are relieved, poverty will instantly be exterminated? Likewise, if one kind of industry is protected today, the number of industries to be protected will inevitably increase tomorrow.[27]

The debate between the two periodicals continued in this way until June 1881, when it stopped abruptly. The reason may be that both sides of the argument had become repetitive and more or less similar in content. *Tokai Keizai Shinpo* ceased publication in October 1882 without prior notice. No contemporary newspaper or magazine made any reference to the closure, with the exception of *Tokyo Keizai Zasshi* which regretted the disappearance of its rival. In spite of such a short span, in comparison with *Tokyo Keizai Zasshi* which lasted until September 1923, *Tokai Keizai Shinpo* left a mark no less indelible than that of its competitor.

8

PROTECTIONISTS ON THE OFFENSIVE

As we saw in Chapter 1, Wakayama Norikazu, in the publisher's preface to the Japanese version (1877) of the English protectionist J. B. Byles's *Sophisms of Free Trade and Popular Political Economy Examined*, used the analogy of a new-born baby, for whom the parents' care is essential, to argue for protective policies.[1] He goes on to say:

> Nowadays it is no longer fashionable among civilized countries to use arms and weapons to subdue other countries. Instead, arts, science, manufactures and means of transport are used to invade overseas markets. The need, therefore, to protect and encourage national industries and thereby to attain commercial advantage cannot be questioned.[2]

As to protective duties, he clearly states:

> It is a long time since I began to think about the need for protective duties. It was in the autumn of 1871 that, following the request of the head of the Department of Taxation, I wrote and submitted the manuscript of *Hogozeisetsu* (On Protective Duties). When I came back from America two years later, it had already been printed and published by the Ministry of Finance, perhaps because recovering autonomy over customs duties on our side had become an issue among the officers concerned.[3]

It was in 1871 that the aforementioned Iwakura Mission was dispatched to discuss the revision of the so-called unequal treaties with America and with the European countries concerned (though with no success). Wakayama was ordered to accompany the Mission to America in order to study financial subjects there. The experience he had there made him the first advocate of life insurance in Japan and one of the earliest purveyors of Western economic thought in the country. Referring to some economic authors of the West, he says with regret:

> As far as I know, the only names of important economic authors that are known to Japanese intellectuals are Adam Smith, J. S. Mill, Francis Wayland, A. L. Perry and the like, all of whom are upholders of free trade principles. They are so alike that only one example of their writing will be sufficient for us to know what they are about. On the other hand, no book advocating protective policies which should suit our actual situation has ever been offered to the public in translation. People might easily believe that free trade is the only doctrine that prevails in Western countries.[4]

As to books by protectionists, Wakayama considers that H. C. Carey's is much too bulky; Sir Edward Sullivan's is too simplified; and the one by E. P. Smith, until recently a government employee, is a little too specific. That is why he has found Byles's book to be suitable for translation:

> In European and American countries scholars and statesmen alike have long been discussing which of the two, protection or freedom, is more preferable for enriching their own country, without ever coming to a solution. . . . It is obvious that political economy is not uniformly applicable everywhere and yet there are some people who never cease to argue that there is a universal principle that applies to all humanity regardless of the situation in which one country is placed differently from others.[5]

Those who hold to the British school of free trade assert that Britain has achieved its supreme wealth and strength because the country has been consistently following that principle by trading with every part of the world. On the contrary, argues Wakayama, Britain has achieved its present wealth and strength because the country never ceased to strive hard to protect its industry for two or three hundred years. This is also the case with France, Germany, Belgium, Switzerland, Denmark, America or indeed any country, because there is not a country known to have become wealthy without ever applying protective policy. Unlike former times it is no longer fashionable in the age of civilization to subdue other countries by force and weapons. The prevailing tactic nowadays is to try to attack and engulf another country's market, using arts and sciences as the general, machines and tools as the stronghold, and the means of transport as the weapon. Thus, for a less advanced country to follow the free trade principle is like 'a crow attempting to imitate a cormorant'.[6]

Even if someone were to try to develop an industry, the result would simply be that his market would easily be undersold and usurped by imports. Who, then, would bother to strive? There is obviously a need for such a market to be protected from imports by means of customs. And yet Japan has no right of its own to exercise such a policy. The reason for translating this book is to inform the public about what the national economy really is. Furthermore, protective policy does not simply mean raising customs duties or limiting imports, it also means encouraging national industry and manufacturing and nourishing the arts and sciences.[7]

It is often claimed by free-traders that a protective policy profits one set of people at the cost of all others, the result of which is to make the rich still richer and the poor even poorer. It will rob people of their birthright, and detract from the benefit of mutual communication. It might look beneficial to the nation in the short run but in the long run it will amount to a decrease in the export of national products, and eventually to a decrease in the national revenue. On the other hand, those who advocate protectionism claim that people cannot live without mutual aid. When a baby is born, it depends on the parents' care. When it grows a little, it cannot do without the instruction of teachers and elders. When it grows up, it depends on the protection of the government. Without the parents' care, starvation will result; without the instruction of teachers and elders knowledge and manners will be lacking; without the protection of the government, violence may ensue. Care by parents, education by teachers, policing by the state are all examples of protection. It is exactly the same with trade, which is essential for the economy.[8]

Which of the above two policies applies to a country depends on the situation in which it is placed. Or, rather, free trade is good in theory but not in practice:

> In such civilized countries as Britain, France and America, there is indeed the theory of free trade but in reality that theory has never been put into practice. In Britain there is a system of monopoly by wealthy merchants. Some goods, such as salt and opium which are produced in East India, are totally monopolized by them. In France it is said that there is a system of

> government monopoly on tobacco. America, too, is said to put heavy duties even on such necessities of life as iron, sugar, tea, salt, cotton wool, etc. to encourage home industry. Without such a practice no country is able to flourish. Thus, it must be even more relevant to Japan.

Japan has for so long followed a policy of isolationism that its people are ignorant of the public interest, unskilled in trade and industry, backward in the arts and manufacturing and in means of transport. 'To enable a country such as Japan to make rapid progress, protective duties must be the best policy to adopt.' By instructing farmers and artisans in what they must do, and by taxing heavily, or even prohibiting, the export of raw produce, arts and manufactures will be encouraged, the idlers will come to find jobs, and the wealthy will know where to employ their capital.[9]

Wakayama's views were shared by Ushiba Takuzo, who argued:

> When an attempt is made to launch something new, it is obvious that some losses will occur. This is because people are not versed in the matters concerned and so are unable to compete with their rivals abroad. Who would dare to do such a thing at their own expense, unless their losses were covered by the government exercising protective duties? Even the free-trader Mr Mill once said that the recent rise in the price of land and produce in America was a result of the rapid growth of industry there. This is enough to prove the effectiveness of the protective system. When the time comes for the treaties to be revised, I trust that Japan will adopt the American style of protective policy, and thereby prevent the outflow of money on the one hand and promote the growth of industry on the other.[10]

Nishimura Shigeki, who later in his career came to be known as a confirmed subscriber to traditional moral doctrine, was interested in economic problems in his earlier days. As a member of the Meiji Six Society, he contributed some articles to its journal, in one of which he defended protectionism. Following on from the paragraph already cited here in Chapter 1, he argues:

> Britain used to have recourse to so-called mercantilism; it levied heavy duties on imports and gave generous grants on exports, thus encouraging its home industries and preventing the out-

> flow of its money. A man by the name of Adam Smith appeared later, in the 1770s, denouncing mercantilism and extolling the benefits of free trade, and since then the latter theory has become predominent in that country. But the fact of the matter, it seems to me, is that it was owing to the mercantilist policy that Britain could achieve enough wealth to carry out free trade later. . . . If Adam Smith had been born years before, I am convinced that he would never have argued for free trade.

Then, referring to America as a country which pursued protectionism, Nishimura concludes that Japan, as a late-starter resembling America, should follow the American way and certainly not the British way.[11]

The works of Wakayama and of Ushiba, and perhaps of Nishimura, probably appeared too early. The time was not yet ripe enough. In contrast, it is no mere coincidence that the publication of Oshima Sadamasu's translation of Friedrich List's *Das nationale System der politischen Oekonomie* (1841) and the promulgation of the Imperial Constitution of Japan took place in the same year, in 1889. It was in the latter half of the 1880s that Oshima, who had once supported economic liberalism and had translated a summarized version of T. R. Malthus's *An Essay on the Principle of Population* in 1877 and W. S. Jevons's *Money and Mechanism of Exchange* in 1883, converted to protectionism. It was as if to mark this conversion that he translated List's book. Then, conforming to List's reasoning, he proceeded to write his own book, *Joseiron* (On the Present Situation) in 1891, the most impressive parts of which are Chapters 2 ('Balance of Trade is most important'), 4 ('To protect Industry is to protect Agriculture'), and 5 ('Free Traders are all short-sighted'). The free-traders' theory of the international division of labour is 'short-sighted', he says, because it sees the national interest only in the short term and not in the long term. It might sound plausible to say that a nation, just like an individual, prefers beauty to ugliness, or cheapness to costliness. But what really matters is not current affluence but the means to produce affluence. Current affluence and cheapness cannot last long unless they are the result of productive power. If there is power to produce things, then future affluence will be realized without fail. Thus, it is undoubtedly more desirable for a nation to nourish the power to produce cheapness and affluence than to be deluded by current beauty and cheapness. In the ensuing chapters he analyses the contemporary Japanese economy and proposes some duties as the means of exercising protectionist policy.

Free-traders claim that money which has flowed out of a country will not fail to flow back again but this applies only between countries whose developmental levels are more or less the same in all ways. Free-traders are also mistaken in their assertion that the protection of industry is a policy which benefits the minority at the expense of the majority, namely the consumers. In a country such as Japan, where the transition from an agricultural to an industrial state is taking place, the protection of industry is essential. The agricultural population are consumers of industrial products, and any benefit to them relies on the progress of industry. The protection of industry, therefore, means the protection of farmers and peasants.

Following the doctrine of Friedrich List, Oshima states:

> When a country which is still in a savage state starts to communicate with other countries, its people, not knowing the benefits of modern industry, should be ready to import the manufactured commodities of foreign countries and to export its raw products, thus learning about mutual interests. At such a stage, a free trade policy should be adopted. By the time that the people have come to appreciate the benefit of trade and to wish to become acquainted with the modern way of manufacturing things, protectionism should be adopted. Once the country has developed modern manufacturing with a solid enough foundation to compete with others, then a free trade policy should again be adopted.[12]

Thus, Oshima believes, it is not a cause for regret that economic liberalism of the British school has prevailed since Japan opened up to the world. But now that, people have grown sufficiently enlightened and their skills in industry and trade have markedly increased, it is high time to change course and to encourage industry by instituting a protective policy. In conclusion he writes:

> It might seem as if the free trade doctrine prevails everywhere. But if one looks around the world, there is no doubt that protectionist theory is far more prevalent. People tend to be attracted by the word 'freedom' but freedom in politics and freedom in foreign trade are entirely different from each other. The former liberates a nation, whereas the latter liberates other nations at the expense of one nation. It is our duty to distinguish between the two theories.[13]

Even if free trade were definitely to be cast off and protectionism were to take over, there would still be a problem. Since Japan has no right of its own to levy customs duties, the choice of free trade over protection is no more than empty talk. Thus, Oshima writes:

> Unless customs rights are restored, there is no way to exercise protection and to promote our industry. In order to restore those rights, the treaties must be revised. . . . In other words, the revision of the treaties must take into account not only legal rights but also customs rights.

As implied here, there were two aspects to the revision of the treaties, namely legal rights and customs rights. As noted in earlier chapters, Japan had no right to prosecute and try foreigners living in Japan, who were under the complete protection of their consulates. When the inequality of the treaties was discussed, greater stress tended to be put on this legal side and it was quite natural for people at large to feel that, without legal rights, Japan could be said to have attained real independence. Nevertheless Oshima, a realist in his economic thinking, goes on to say that 'from the point of view of the national interest, it is evident that customs rights are far more important than legal rights'.[14]

9

THE IMPERIAL CONSTITUTION

It is not entirely clear how the Japanese people came to know that in the Western world there was something like a Constitution which served as the basis of all legal regulations within each country. The first opportunity might well have been when Fukuzawa Yukichi's bestseller *Seiyo Jijo, Shohen* (Conditions in the West, vol. 1) was published in 1866, two years before the Meiji Restoration. The book was, as mentioned before, a translation of a number of sources assembled by Fukuzawa in order to inform his compatriots about the realities of so-called Western civilization. For example, the book says that, in Britain, there is no class discrimination between *samurai* and non-*samurai*, the government never interferes with the religion of individuals, and the right of the monarch to rule over his or her country is checked by laws passed by both Houses of Parliament. Fukuzawa also included in the book his translation of the American Declaration of Independence, as an example of a document ensuring all sorts of freedom for the citizens of the country.[1]

Far less impressive and less widely read, yet much more systematic, was a book published by Tsuda Mamichi in the last year of the Tokugawa period. *Taisei Kokuhoron* (On the Laws in the West) was a translation of the legal parts of a series of lectures given by Professor Simon Vissering of Leiden University in Holland. As mentioned in earlier chapters, both Tsuda and his colleague Nishi Amane were private students of Vissering, having been sent to the University by the Shogunate. The book enumerates a number of basic rights and freedoms which every individual has with regard to the state. It says, for example, that, when a monarch behaves unlawfully, his or her subjects are allowed to decline to obey his or her orders and are justified in doing so, and that the extent of the refusal varies according to the degree of unlawfulness, ranging from simple rejection to actual revolution.[2] The Imperial Constitution of Japan which was to emerge over twenty years later had no such element in it. However, there was still a very long way to go from such early encounters with the idea of a constitution to the actual enactment. Many things happened in between.

The first notable move was a proposition which was submitted to the government in 1874 by eight distinguished figures (Soejima Taneomi, Goto Shojiro, Itagaki Taisuke, Eto Shinpei, Yuri Kosei, Komoro Nobuo, Okamoto Kenzaburo and Furusawa Shigeru). The 'Proposal for establishing a Diet based on Popular Election' presented its case as follows:

> In Japan at present political power does not rest with the emperor or with the people. All power belongs to the government. This is not right. The proper state of affairs consists in the establishment of a Diet based on election, because those who are obliged to pay taxes to the government ought to be entitled to become acquainted with the policies of the government. It is often claimed that the people are not yet sufficiently educated and consequently too immature to participate in politics. Such an argument is mistaken. The best way to educate the people is to let them participate in public affairs. It is sheer arrogance to say that the Diet is simply an assembly of fools. The task of the government is to encourage people to progress in all possible ways. In savage and primitive ages when people were too brave to be obedient, the duty of the government was to teach them how to obey. Japan is no longer in such a savage state and yet people are still much too obedient. They need to become emboldened and to understand their public duty. Therefore a Diet based on popular election should be established, so that they may become accustomed to participating in public affairs.[3]

It might well be said that this argument should not be accepted at face value, because it was mooted by people who had the previous year sided with those in favour of a war with Korea and had been defeated on the issue. Even so, viewed objectively, their argument played a vital role in the process.

The proposition was immediately rejected by some notable people, such as Kato Hiroyuki. According to him, the Diet was an institution for making laws and, in order to make laws, a number of qualified people had to be elected. To elect qualified people was not an easy task, and was one which should be undertaken only by the intelligent and educated. Currently, however, people at large were neither intelligent nor educated. Frederick the Great of Prussia was so enlightened that he unilaterally rejected despotism, despite its being common elsewhere, and personally revised the law so that the imperial power might be limited, but he never went as far as to institute a Diet. The reason was that people were not enlightened enough to take part in politics. For the same reason Russia had no Diet. Was Japan to have what Russia did not yet have? It was true that the authorities ought not be so arrogant as to regard themselves as being wiser than their people, but the number of intelligent people in the country could possibly be more than a few dozen out of a population of thirty million. In order to make people conscious of their duty to share public responsibility, merely establishing a Diet would not be sufficient. Much more urgent was the education of the people through the construction of schools, for which time was needed. Prussia had become a European power not because it had established a Diet in early times but because it had tried to cultivate its people's capabilities by means of education.[4]

Kato had already published, in 1872, an abridged translation of a book by Johann C. Bluntchli entitled *Kokuho Hanron* (General Theory of Law). This is believed to have influenced Inoue Kowashi who was to become a central figure in the drafting of the Constitution. Kato naturally objected to the proposition because it was so much at odds with German legal ideas.

Although it is quite understandable that a conservative such as Kato should be critical of the proposition, it may seem unnatural that the leading figures in the Meiji Enlightenment such as Nishi Amane and Mori Arinori were also opposed, whereas an economic protectionist such as Nishimura Shigeki was in favour. Nishi's criticism of the proposition runs as follows. Politics and physics are not the same. The law of gravitation in Britain is exactly the same as that in France. Electricity works by exactly the same law in America as in Japan. But such is not the case with politics. On the contrary, the parliament in Britain is different from that in France. The form of government in Britain and that in France are just as different from each other as fire and water are. To claim that taxpayers are entitled to share in national policy-making is wrong. Tax-payment is one thing; political participation is quite another. They do not necessarily go hand in hand. For example, in the theatre, the right order of things is to practise first and then to act on the stage afterwards. To practise after raising the curtain would be a topsy-turvy way of proceeding. In the case of plays, the worst outcome might be only that the audience stops coming. But politics is not like that. It is not appropriate, therefore, to regard the Diet as a place for practice and education.[5]

Mori was even more cynical. He pointed out that those who signed the proposition were responsible, because they held government offices at the time, for issuing the newspaper ordinance that prohibited any anti-government journalism. How could they justify their argument for establishing a Diet?[6] Such a response was quite natural because, even after the establishment of the Diet had been announced, Mori's attitudes towards a constitution in Japan were still negative. Interviewed by a journalist in England in February 1884, at the close of his four-year post as Ambassador in London, Mori said: 'It is true that in 1890 a Parliament is to meet in Japan, and that we have been steadily, but tentatively, progressing in the direction of parliamentary institutions. We have, for instance, city and provincial assemblies. . . . But I doubt whether parliamentarism can be successfully grafted upon Japanese habits of thought. It is hardly in the natural line of our historical development.'[7] These views must have owed much to the influence of Herbert Spencer whom he used to meet regularly in the latter's favourite club.[8]

Nishimura's argument, on the other hand, was as follows:

> Everything has two sides, theoretical and practical. Some things are good in theory but bad in practice; others are the other way round. But there are things which are good in both and which are applicable at any time and in any country without ever causing harm. As to the matter of the Diet, its theory is impartial and its practice is clearly exemplified by the wealth and strength of European countries. The argument of Soejima and others may sound radical, but radicalism is of two kinds, good and bad. The radicalism that caused Washington and Jefferson to revolt against Britain was good, whereas the radicalism that led Robespierre and Danton to bring down the French monarchy was bad. The argument for the Diet is the good aspect of radicalism. To claim that people are still not intelligent enough to set up a Diet is also wrong. It was as early as the thirteenth century that people gathered openly to discuss public affairs in England. The English of six hundred years ago cannot be supposed to have been more intelligent than Japanese people of today. And what have the English achieved ever since through parliamentary debates and

enactments? It is not so much too early as too late for us to establish our Diet.[9]

The government ignored the proposition. Instead, an imperial order was issued to the Genroin, or Senate, two years later in 1876, commanding that a Constitution be drafted. It took four years for the Genroin to complete the draft, which turned out to be too pro-British in appearance. First, the civil list had to be resolved in the Diet; second, the Emperor, the Genroin and the Diet were made jointly responsible for law-making, an idea copied from the British system of 'King in Parliament'; and third, the Emperor was to swear at the time of his succession faithfully to keep the Constitution, which again was a copy of the British system, an example of the compact between the monarch and his or her people.[10]

The leading members of the government, Iwakura Tomomi and Ito Hirobumi, flatly declared that the draft was nothing more than a reproduction of some of the European constitutions that they had gathered and modified and that it was much too superficial, giving little or no consideration to the future peace and interest of the nation.[11] Their inclination towards German ideas goes back to the period from November 1871 to September 1873 when the aforementioned Iwakura Mission, with Ito as a member, visited a number of Western countries, namely America, Britain, France, Belgium, Holland, Germany, Russia, Denmark, Sweden, Italy, Austria and Switzerland. The influence of Germany proved to have the strongest effect after they met Wilhelm I, Bismark, Moltke and others.[12] Thus, it was not unexpected that the Genroin draft did not impress them. Okuma Shigenobu, known for his inclination towards the British political system, was forced to resign from the government in 1881. This led to his organizing, in the following year, the second of the early political parties in Japan, the Rikken Kaishinto (Constitutional Reform Party). The first, Itagaki Taisuke's Jiyuto (Liberal Party), was founded in 1881.

Iwakura and Ito entrusted Inoue Kowashi with the task of writing the alternative draft.[13] At the same time they had an imperial declaration issued which said that the Diet was to be called in 1890. Their intention apparently was to nullify the popular arguments for the Constitution that were then at their height. A movement for political modernization, called the Freedom and People's Rights Movement, or Jiyu Minken Undo, had begun as early as 1875 and reached its peak in 1880–1.[14]

At the annual general meeting of an organization called the League for the Diet, formed in 1880, those who were present discussed the need for a Diet and a Constitution and resolved that at the next meeting, to be held the following year, each local member society would present its draft of the Constitution. Local societies were mostly formed from the middle-class intelligentsia, consisting of the wealthier farmers and merchants. However, after the political crisis of 1881, in which Okuma had to resign, the situation was changed completely by the so-called deflationary financial policy of the then financial minister Matsukata Masayoshi, and the subsequent oppressive policies of the government. Local uprisings against the government's policies took place in various districts but they were easily suppressed.

Meanwhile, over thirty drafts for a Constitution were produced by different societies. (As recently as 1968, in the long-disused barn of a former land-owning family in a far-western rural part of Tokyo Prefecture, some historians discovered a draft consisting of 204 articles drawn up by an assistant teacher at a local primary school and his society. It is quite possible that something else of the kind may be discovered in some other parts of the country to add to the known number of drafts.) It is worth noting that most of the drafts, with perhaps the exception of Ueki Emori's draft based on a republican principle, were mildly monarchical. Even these were severely suppressed. When the first penal law was enacted in 1882, it retained the essence of all of the foregoing oppressive ordinances, such as those prohibiting impropriety towards the Emperor, the Imperial families and even the government officers, those regulating newspapers and those prohibiting public meetings.

In 1882 Ito himself went to Europe in order to gather necessary information about various constitutions, but mainly German. That which impressed him most was the Prussian. Out of the thirteen months that he was away from Japan, he spent as many as eight in Germany and Austria. When he returned to Japan in the following year, he found that Iwakura had just died. Thus, it was Ito and Inoue who came to play the most important roles in Constitution-making. In 1884 the Department for the Preparation of the Constitution was instituted in the Imperial Court. In 1885 the Genroin was almost abolished (though the actual abolition did not occur until 1890) and the Cabinet took over most of its business. Meanwhile, the drafting of the Constitution by Inoue officially started in 1886. The completed draft was forwarded to the newly established Privy Council, which made some alterations, and the Emperor promulgated the Constitution in 1889.

When Inoue started his constitutional study in 1881, he consulted the legal adviser to the Genroin, Gustave Emile Boissonade de Fontarabie. Boissonade had been a teacher at the government's law school since 1874, and Inoue had been a student of his while studying law in France in 1872. Inoue asked Boissonade which of the three options he believed to be the best: supreme power in a monarch, as in the Constitution of the German State of Württemburg; supreme power in the people, as in the French Constitution; or the intermediate way of sharing the power between monarch and people. Boissonade immediately replied by letter as follows. Neither in the Württemburg Constitution of 1819 nor in the Bavarian Constitution of 1811 did the crown assume absolute sovereignity. Although it was true that in Article 4 of the Württemburg Constitution the monarch was the head of the state, on reading the Constitution as a whole it was clear that there were two national assemblies to share the power with the crown. It was by and large the same in the Bavarian Constitution. In the French Constitution of 1814, Article 13 stated that the king was the head of the country, but Article 14 immediately defined the two national assemblies as having power along with the king. Here, too, in public affairs, especially in the matter of taxation, the participation of the people through the assembly was clear enough. The king was thus the head of the administrative power, so that it was not right to call the sharing of power between the crown and the people an intermediate theory. In most countries, such as Italy, Spain, Portugal, Austria, Germany, Sweden, Norway, Denmark, Holland, Great Britain and Belgium, the King or Queen shared the power with the national assembly. Despotism was found only in Russia and Turkey. But Russia might become a constitutional country before long and Turkey would not last very long as an independent country. Republicanism existed only in France and Switzerland. So the question, Boissonade continued, should rather be which of these three might be the best: constitutional monarchy, despotism or republicanism. Despotism was out of the question. The republican system applied to a country such as France which had experienced, and yet had not been satisfied with, despotism, monarchy, and empire; it did not apply to a country such as Japan which had kept the emperor at its head for 2,500 years. But, since it had been generally accepted abroad that people who have the duty of military service and of tax-paying should also have the right to decide those matters, imperial despotism was no longer possible. In Boissonade's view, the Emperor's recent undertaking to establish a Diet proved the point.[15]

Boissonade's advice was apparently not carried into effect. Among the Inoue Papers there is, along with Boissonade's, a document which is a draft of the preamble of the Constitution.[16] It was written by Hermann Roesler, a German who had been in Japan as a legal adviser to the government since 1879.[17] It is very likely that he wrote for Inoue not only the preamble but also the whole text; but only the preamble still exists. Almost all of the preamble was adopted into Inoue's draft, written in 1887–8 at Prime Minister Ito's request, though the part referring to the freedom of the press, assembly, security of persons and property, and so on was discarded. Instead, those items were shown as part of the Emperor's grace from above, because Inoue's preamble says that the Emperor will protect the security of the person and property of his subjects so long as that security does not become inconsistent with interest of the whole nation, and that he wishes that his subjects may enjoy both public and private rights.

In Inoue's, and therefore Roesler's, preamble, sovereign power rests with the Emperor and no one else. The sanctioning of laws, the appointment of civil and military servants, conscription, the decision for or against war and peace, the concluding of treaties, diplomatic relations with foreign countries, and all similar matters belong to the powers of the Emperor. The concluding part of the preamble states that present and future subjects ought to be as faithful to the Constitution as to the Emperor and his heirs.

In this way, the birth of the Imperial Constitution was a process, akin to the Franco–German war; an ideological war on the Japanese Constitution to come, fought, it might be said, on the battlefield of political principles in the dawn of Japanese modernization. The one lost and the other won. It paralleled the battle between the economic principles of free trade and protection.

Nakae Chomin, a left-wing democrat who had studied in France and had been so influenced by J. J. Rousseau's thought as to be called 'the Rousseau of the Orient', demanded in 1890:

> What have we been given by the Constitution? What power does the Diet have? What does the Cabinet owe to the Diet? What participation do people have in the matter of treaties or war and peace? Are not our people going to be the government's slaves?[18]

The Constitution, despite all of its German elements, contains purely Japanese characterisics, especially those concerning the Emperor. As early as 1874 or 1875, soon after returning from France, Inoue wrote an article entitled 'We should not blindly follow Europe', in which he stressed the need for national identity. It is likely that he found that identity in one of the Japanese classics, *Jinno Shotoki* (Holy Emperors in Authentic Succession) written by Kitabatake Chikafusa in 1339, which claims, as the title suggests, that the Japanese Emperors are holy and ought to be in eternal succession. Thus, the first article of the Constitution, which virtually duplicates the first article of Inoue's draft, declares that the Great Empire of Japan is ruled over by the uninterrupted succession of Emperors; the second article affirms that the Emperor is sacred and inviolable. Although it is not explicitly stated, the Emperor is made a living god.

For that reason the Showa Emperor, well over half a century later, that is, after the Japanese surrender to the allied forces in World War II, had to make the so-called 'human declaration', denying that he was a living god. The Bill for a completely revised Constitution, which was drawn up under external pressure from the occupation authorities, passed the Diet in October 1946 and was promulgated the following month. The Emperor no longer had sovereign power and the rights of the people were secured. Conditions have continued to change drastically ever since.

It was recently proved, however, that elements of the Old Constitution, of emperor worship, still survived in spite of all of the changes in the time since the inception of the so-called New Constitution. These elements were apparent after the last Emperor, Showa Emperor, fell seriously ill and they came to their height when he eventually died. During that period, television and radio and every national newspaper and magazine were full of items relating to him, his family and the Showa era. Books were placed on long tables set up outside the gates to the palace. Every day people queued to sign the books to express their wish for his early recovery and then, when he died, for his peaceful rest. At his death, not only central and local government offices but also department stores, shops, theatres and concert halls, schools, colleges and universities (with a very few exceptions) were closed. Private television stations stopped commercial advertisements completely. It was as unexpected as it was extraordinary. A kind of morally enforced calm prevailed everywhere. Even to some of those who were old enough to have lived under both Old and New Constitutions, it was an amazing state of affairs. Only three months after the death of the Showa Emperor, it was reported that the number of people taking the trouble to visit his grave in a very remote part of Tokyo Prefecture, in order to pray for him, had been as large as 450,000 and was rising.

APPENDIX

Enlightenment by translation: Fukuzawa as a translator

Fukuzawa began his career as a translator as a civil servant in charge of the translation of official documents in Dutch for the Shogunate government. Afterwards, as a freelance translator, he worked on English texts. As he says in his fascinating *Fukuo Jiden* (Fukuzawa's Autobiography), the period just before and after the Restoration was the time when he worked hardest at writing and translating.[1] His activities then were indeed remarkable.

Though he says 'writing and translating', the proportion of the latter was much greater than the former in the publications that he produced during that spell. On the other hand, his activities as an author continued until towards the end of his life, while those as a translator covered only the period from 1866 to 1874, from the publication of *Seiyo Jijo, Shohen* (Conditions in the West, vol. 1) to that of *Choai no Ho* (A Guide to Bookkeeping), and peaked in 1869 with the greatest number of publications. What, then, characterized his translating activities which provided, in spite of their brief span, the core of his thought thereafter?

Two facets of Fukuzawa's activities are certainly worthy of interest in themselves: first, how he managed to deal successfully with so many things, such as liberty, rights, and competition, for which there were no corresponding concepts in Japan and, second, the extent to which the words and phrases that he invented in order to express matters which had not existed in Japan passed into common use. Unfortunately, however, this Appendix must be concerned only with Fukuzawa's attitude to translation and the spirit underlying it.

Although *Seiyo Jijo* has often, strangely enough, been taken for Fukuzawa's own writing, he clearly states that it is a translation and describes his motives for taking up the texts included. Having read some books published in Britain and America on history and geography, he says, he made a summarized translation of those which concerned Western countries. Although it was some time since Western books had started to enter Japan and some had already been translated, most of them pertained to literature, arts and technology, and not the custom, politics, and economy that had given birth to them. Fukuzawa realized in the course of translating work, that political and economic renovation or Westernization, is more basic and essential than the mere learning or copying of the piecemeal fruits of civilization such as railways, electricity and gas and water supply.

This does not mean that he intended that his work should have lasting value. On the contrary, he says that some people had kindly advised him to refine his style, by asking for the help of those who specialized in classical literature, so that the work on which he was engaged might attain the permanency that it deserved. However, such a step, he believed, would negate the very purpose of his translations, which was to have them understood as easily, as quickly and as widely as possible. This shows the character of his spirit of enlightenment.

The same spirit is found in the order of translation of the three volumes of *Seiyo Jijo*. At the beginning of the first volume Fukuzawa listed the contents of both volumes (only two were originally intended): in volume 1, politics, taxation, the steam-engine, railways, the telegraph and gaslight in Book I, the United States of America and Holland in Book II, and Britain in Book III, in volume 2, Russia in Book IV, France in Book V, and Portugal, Germany and Prussia in Book VI. However, the intended volume 2 was postponed; it became volume 3 and the contents were altered, so that Portugal, Germany and Prussia were dropped and replaced by human rights and taxation. An extra volume was added in between. Fukuzawa, on returning from America in 1867, explained the reason for the change:

> To follow the original contents, as shown in volume 1 would be to give the reader piecemeal historical and political facts for a few different countries without first providing the background information that is common to them all. It is like seeing the layout of a house without knowing its construction. This is why I have taken up Chambers's *Political Economy* with some additions from other sources.[2]

This change of plan is in accordance with his original proposition, as seen above, that it is better to learn about basic history, politics and economy, which gave birth to the fruits of civilization, than about the mere fruits themselves.

The other side to his attitude towards enlightment, that is to say, the call to answer the immediate need of the day rather than to seek lasting value, is also apparent in the new volume 2. As already noted here in Chapter 4, Fukuzawa claimed that the latter half of the Chambers's book was by and large the same as William Ellis's *Outlines of Social Economy*, which had been translated by his friend Kanda Takahira, and that that was why he was skipping over it. He wrote:

> It is not because I want to save energy that I am refraining from translating the whole of this book. As civilization proceeds, translated books appear one after the other, and yet it is obviously impossible either to translate all books or to read all translated books. Therefore, it is better to spare the energy for the translation of some other new and useful book, and thereby to offer it for the use of society, than to spend the energy in vain over a book which is more or less the same.[3]

A similar attitude is found in a book entitled *Seiyo Ryoko Annai* (A Guide to Western Trips) which was published in the same year, 1867, and is typical of Fukuzawa in this period. He says: 'The shape of the world is round like a ball. So it is called "globe", meaning earth ball. In that globe there are seas and lands. Lands consist of five Continents: Asian, European, . . .'. The book contains the experiences he had during his third overseas tour and on his second visit to America in the same year; the memorandum or diary that he wrote at the time of his European tour; and the summarized translation of some foreign books. Therefore, the book is only partly translation but the object of its publication has something in common with that of his other translated books. In the preface he refers to his motive for compiling the book:

> This booklet is for those who know nothing about foreign countries, so that it will be of no interest or use to those who have already read books on those countries or have actually been there. My wish is that the number of people who will become well acquainted with things Western and who will consequently not need a book such as this might increase.[4]

Though expressed in a different way, the implication here is exactly the same as that in *Seiyo Jijo, Shohen* in which he said, as described in Chapter 4, that his translation would before too long prove to be elementary nonsense. His sincere wish was simply to enlighten people.

Another example of the driving force behind Fukuzawa's bid to enlighten lies in the preface to *Keimo Tenarai no Bun* (Enlightening Penmanship, 1871). It says that the ratio of pupils to the whole population is 1:77 in Russia, where the degree of popularization of education is the lowest among European countries, and 1:8 in Holland, where education is most widely spread. If Japan were to aim at an average figure between the two, by promulgating the Law of Education, the ratio would be 1:42. If the population of Japan was approximately 40,000,000, then the supposed number of pupils would be 940,000. Assuming that the average cost for education per head would be 100 yen per year, then the total cost would be at least 94,000,000 yen, a sum currently far beyond reach. Thus, the best possible interim measure would be to have as many writing masters as possible use this booklet as a textbook. For too long their textbooks had had nothing to do with real learning, since only Japanese and Chinese classical poems and prose had traditionally been used.

This line of thought that, since the spread of school education would take some time, the most effective expedient meanwhile would be to utilize the ubiquitous writing masters, is found elsewhere in his work. The unpublished note 'Tojin Orai' (Foreigners In and Out, 1865) says that the duty of those who are engaged in Western studies is to help the Japanese nation to change, so that they may participate in civilization and culture as soon as possible.[5]

The original text of the preface to the book that Fukuzawa translated and published in 1875, under the title of *Choai no Ho* (A Guide to Bookkeeping), states:

> In estimating the true basis of any science, it is well, if possible, to follow the line of its history, and become familiar with the order and processes of its development. This is especially true of the science of bookkeeping, for although it is purely a branch of mathematics, and as such fully entitled to the favor and consideration of scientific men, yet at no period of its history has it ranked, in the estimation of scholars, with the more complex and abstract sciences; which fact is owing, mainly, to a misconception or under appreciation of its dignity and importance as connected with the actual duties of life. It is lamentably

> true that men will grow enthusiastic over the solution of a problem in Euclid, or the movements upon a chess-board, who are ignorant of the first principles of this the most beautiful and practical of sciences; and are content to pass through life, receiving and appropriating the reputation belonging to men of science and erudition, while they are consciously and persistently unable to decide the simplest question in partnership settlements, or to appreciate the well-established theory of debits and credits in any of its practical applications or philosophical abstractions.[6]

Fukuzawa's translation of this is so much in his own style that it could easily be mistaken for his own work instead of a translation. How he acquired such a mastery of English as well as of a subject completely strange to him is a mystery.

It is estimated that the number of people who were able to go to study in Western countries during the seven years prior to the demise of the Shogunate, i.e. from 1860 to 1867, was about 150. Fukuzawa was not among this number, so it is all the more impressive that he could grasp the essence of the text and translate it so lucidly. No doubt this owed much to his natural talent but it must also have resulted from his eagerness to spread enlightenment. His translation is certainly reminiscent of his appreciation of 'real learning' and his dismissal of 'vain learning'.

Along with the translation of the author's preface is a translator's introduction, the opening section of which was quoted in Chapter 5.[7] In this Fukuzawa expresses the wish that both the learned and the wealthy should, by means of his translation, discover what the real learning of the West is, thereby leading to the reformation of the national economy and to the increase in power of the country. Whether or not the phrase 'the power of the country' is indicative of his nationalism may need further corroboration, but his defence of 'real learning' is clear enough. On that point he continues:

> For hundreds of years in Japan the scholars of Japanese and Chinese studies have concerned themselves solely with vain learning, and thus have looked down on people at large. Peasants, artisans and tradesmen have all had their fill of the scholars' behaviour, to the extent that they want nothing to do with learning, whether vain or real. This has proved to be a great obstacle to the spread of Western learning in an attempt to

> bring about progress. If this manual on bookkeeping were to be used as a textbook in schools and consequently if pupils were to talk about it at home, their parents would soon realize that Western learning is real learning and the number of people letting their children study it would increase. Thus, this booklet would not merely teach the art of bookkeeping but would also lead to a rise in the number of those entering the sphere of real learning in general. If this booklet could extirpate the heinous crime committed by past and present scholars of vain learning, by which they made fools of people, and so could lead peasants, artisans and tradesmen towards enlightenment, then all of the trouble taken to translate this text would be well rewarded.[8]

Here we see both the self-confidence and the aspirations of Fukuzawa as a promoter of enlightenment. Immediately preceding the above quotation there is a passage which says that 'in Japan, since olden times, learning and manual labour have had nothing to do with each other' and that 'peasants and tradesmen respect scholars outwardly but despise them inwardly, so that they very often prohibit their children from reading books'.[9] This resembles the opening part of the first book of *Gakumon no Susume* (Encouragement of Learning, 1872). After the famous passage that 'all people are born equal', and that 'no one is born nobler or meaner than another', it is said that 'since ancient times there have been few scholars who are both learned and good at manual tasks and, conversely, there have been few tradesmen who are fond of poems and yet good at their business, so that peasants and tradesmen do not like to see their children fond of studying.'[10]

These two passages, the one in *Choai no Ho* and the other in *Gakumon no Susume*, are so alike as to be almost a repetition. It could be said that *Gakumon no Susume* was the principle and *Choai no Ho* was its application. They were born of the same spirit.

Fukuzawa's concern is demonstrated at a more practical level. For instance, in the 'Day Book' the price of each piece of cloth, such as 20 dollars and 15 dollars, is expressed simply as 20 yen and 15 yen, instead of in the equivalent sums in Japanese currency calculated at the current exchange rate. Likewise, the length of each piece of cloth, such as 10 yards and 20 yards, is expressed, not in the exact equivalents, but in the round number of Japanese units. In addition, the kinds of cloth, such as broad cloth, cassimere and black dress silk, are expressed as varieties more familiar to the Japanese reader, and the name of each dealer is paraphrased, turning John Smith into Yamato-ya, James Monroe into Kawachi-ya, etc. All of this is done to make things easier for the reader. Even so, Fukuzawa believes that the book is a literal, not a free, translation of the original text. Similarly, in the similar case of the translation of an introductory guide to physical sciences, he states explicitly in the preface: 'Changes from things Western to things Japanese have been made in order to give the reader easier access but no change has been made to the text itself'.[11]

An interesting series of events sheds light on both Fukuzawa's person and his grasp of English. As discussed in Chapter 5, when the first commercial school was opened in Japan, an American by the name of William C. Whitney was invited to teach some commercial subjects there. He closed his own commercial college at Newark and travelled with his family to Japan. His fourteen-year old daughter, Clara, kept a remarkable diary of her stay and seems to have had the opportunity to meet Fukuzawa from time to time. About one such instance she writes:

> On the way back I stopped at Mr Fukuzawa's. . . . He has an entirely Japanese house now, but as clean as a pin. Mr Fukuzawa is always kind to me and I admire him truly. He is so strong and manly, and he has translated so many good books into Japanese. His school is very celebrated for debates and he is exceedingly liberal-minded.[12]

The word 'debates' relates to Fukuzawa's belief in democracy and enlightenment. He was convinced that one of the defects of Japanese tradition lay in the fact that there was no custom of open speech and debate, so he had a house built at his school which was used exclusively as a debating chamber. The house still stands in the campus of Keio University, the latter day descendant of the school.

Clara also refers to a meeting where a number of prominent figures gathered, including Fukuzawa:

> Mr Nakamura (Masanao), in a swallow-tail several sizes too large for him and an unruly collar, beamed upon us from behind a door, where the crowd forced his insignificant figure. The tall, muscular form of Mr Fukuzawa, arrayed in the stiffest of stiff *hakama*, towered above the surrounding men of shorter stature. He looked very pleased at seeing us and gave us a low salaam and a grunt of welcome. He was the only gentleman present in the Japanese dress, but I cannot but confess that he looked far

> more dignified and at ease in his handsome robes than did those loose-jointed, heated gentlemen in ill-fitting European dress. Mr Fukuzawa has undergone a complete revolution in his ideas, for he not only discarded his European house and style of living, but he no longer wears foreign clothes, or uses our forms of salutation. Still, he is as he ever has been, my favorite among the three noted teachers of Tokyo. He is a bear – but a kindly one.[13]

Even more intriguing is her reference to Fukuzawa's English:

> Mr Fukuzawa has a comical way of speaking, using English and Japanese in the utmost confusion, so that it is difficult to understand what he really means. For example, speaking of the Governor: 'Mr Kuriyama is *honto ni* [very] kind man, *keredomo* [but] he is *taiso* [extremely] busy *kono setsu* [of late], yes?'[14]

In contrast to his clumsiness in spoken English, with its Japanese mannerism, his mastery of English as a whole and his unabated devotion to Westernization and civilization are all the more impressive.

But why so much Westernization? There is an unpublished essay written in 1870. It is concerned not with translation directly but with private schools to teach Western subjects. However, since the aim of both translation and schools for Western teaching was to spread Western, and so 'real', studies, his views on such schools have much in common with his views on translation.

> Education is the very foundation of the country. For the enhancement of people's virtue and knowledge, and for the growth in wealth and strength of the country, nothing can be better than education. Among the foreigners there are unprincipled rogues who look down on us as if we were Eskimos and who try to profit by keeping us poor and ignorant. They do not welcome our seeking civilization and culture; they are content if we indulge only in Japanese and Chinese studies, concentrating only on the old and impractical. What they would most dislike now would be for us to incline towards Western studies. They would be obliged to stop regarding us as if we were Eskimos if we were to start reading Western books, to get to know Western circumstances, and to talk about world affairs. That is why we are in urgent need of Western studies, regardless of the merits or demerits of the three kinds of studies,

> namely Japanese, Chinese and Western. Once we have appreciated the urgent need for Western studies, we must try to disseminate them. In order to do so, we must think of the country as a whole; we must disregard the distinction between public and private institutions and consider only the progress or decline of Western studies within the entire country.[15]

As the conclusion to this might suggest, it was written in order to denounce the current attempt to improve public schools at the expense of private schools, and so was not directly intended to defend the significance of Western studies or the translation of Western books. However, the assertion that most foreigners were displeased with the Japanese aiming at 'civilization and culture' but content with the Japanese being absorbed in traditional Japanese and Chinese studies or, in his phraseology, in vain learning instead of real learning, is of interest. The spread of Western studies, and so of 'civilization and culture', is explicitly related here to the need for the nation to confront foreigners.

A very similar statement is found in another unpublished essay, 'Tojin Orai' (Foreigners In and Out), written four or five years before:

> Whether a country is strong or weak, big or small, depends on the size of population. In that sense Japan is greater than most other countries of the world. . . . From the geographical point of view, Japan is almost next to nothing, occupying no more than a three-hundredth part of the earth, but from the point of view of population it comprises a thirtieth part of the whole world. In addition, Japan is richly provided with natural products, not merely food but gold, silver, copper and many other minerals, and so should not be afraid of any foreign country.[16]

And yet, he continues, Japan has been closed to the outer world for so long. While enjoying internal peace, it has let time pass by without noticing that railways, steamships, cannons, rifles and the like have been invented in foreign countries.

> With regard to education and the military arts, having read only Japanese and Chinese books and relied only on swords, spears and the like, the Japanese are now trailing so far behind foreigners that they are obliged to shiver at the threat of the menace from outside. Therefore, it is high time, if not already too late, for us to make up our mind, to set aside Chinese studies

> and spears and swords, and to learn European ways, making steamships, cannons and rifles. ... If any foreign country should ever come to attack us, then we will be justified in driving it away by force.[17]

The reason behind this call to part with the traditional way of life and to adopt the new European way is clear. Similarly, the intention behind the spreading of 'real learning' through the book of book-keeping, and so reforming the national economy and thereby increasing the power of the nation, is evident. It was precisely this element which constituted the essential attitude of Fukuzawa towards translating Western books. For Fukuzawa, even before he became a prolific author, enlightenment was fused with nationalism.

NOTES

PREFACE

1 Carmen Blacker, *The Japanese Enlightenment: A Study of the Writings of Fukuzawa Yukichi*, Cambridge, 1964.
2 R. H. Havens, *Nishi Amane and Modern Japanese Thought*, Princeton, 1970, p. 3.

1 THE DEVELOPMENT OF ECONOMIC THOUGHT IN MEIJI JAPAN

1 For the economic thought of Sada as a whole, see E. Honjo, *Nihon Keizai Shisoshi* (History of Economic Thought in Japan), Tokyo, 1966, vol. 2, pp. 265–314. Sada's main economic work, *Saibai Keizairon*, Tokyo, 1878, is included in *Meiji Bunka Zenshu* (Collected Works of Meiji Culture: hereafter *MBZ*), Tokyo, 1929, vol. 15, pp. 307–410.
2 The rather symbolic experience of Fukuzawa at Yokohama, which he visited in 1859 to see the changes in the town since its port had been opened to some Western countries, may be cited here:

> I had been striving with all my powers for many years to learn the Dutch books. And now, with regard to Dutch studies, I had reason to believe that I was one of the best in the country, and yet I found that I could not even read the signs of merchants who had come from foreign lands to trade with us. . . . Those signs must have been in either English or French – probably English, for I had had inklings that English was the language most widely used in the world. A treaty with the two English-speaking countries had just been concluded. As certain as day, English was to be the most useful language of the future. . . . In my disappointment my spirit was low, but I knew that it was not the time to be sitting still. (Y. Fukuzawa, *Fukuo Jiden* [Fukuzawa's Autobiography], Tokyo, 1899; English translation by E. Kiyooka, Tokyo, 1934, revised edn 1960, p. 98. [In citing, some modifications have been made to Kiyooka's text.])

3 T. Kanda, *Denzei Shinpo* (New Land Tax proposed), 1872; *MBZ*, 1929, vol. 9, pp. 505–8.

4 The phrase is taken from the title of Carmen Blacker's *The Japanese Enlightenment: A Study of the Writings of Fukuzawa Yukichi*, Cambridge, 1964.
5 *Chambers's Educational Course: Political Economy, for Use in Schools, and for Private Instruction*, London and Edinburgh, 1873 edn, p. 49. For both the author and the date of impression (1852) of this book, see A. M. Craig, 'John Hill Burton and Fukuzawa Yukichi', *Kindai Nihon Kenkyu* (Journal for the Study of Modern Japan), Keio University Fukuzawa Research Centre, Tokyo, 1984, vol. 1.
6 *Chambers's Educational Course: Political Economy*, p. 38.
7 Y. Fukuzawa, *Minkan Keizairoku* (Popular Political Economy), Tokyo, 1878, vol. 1; 1881, vol. 2. *Fukuzawa Yukichi Zenshu* (Complete Works of Fukuzawa Yukichi), Tokyo, 1958–63, vol. 4, pp. 373–7.
8 H. Kato, *Koeki Mondo* (A Dialogue on Trade), Tokyo, 1869; *MBZ*, vol. 9, pp. 57–74.
9 T. Amano, *Keizai Genron* (Principles of Political Economy), Tokyo, 1886, pp. 13–14.
10 Ibid., pp. 17–19.
11 M. Tsuda, 'Hogozei o Hitosuru Setsu' (Protective Duties Criticized), *Meiroku Zasshi* (Meiji Six Journal), no. 5, 1874; *MBZ*, 1928, vol. 18, pp. 72–4.
12 Preface to M. Hayashi, *Keizai Benmo* (Economic Misunderstandings Corrected), Tokyo, 1878.
13 Ibid., p. 1.
14 N. Wakayama, *Hogozeisetsu* (On Protective Duties), Tokyo, 1871; *Wakayama Norikazu Zenshu* (Complete Works of Wakayama Norikazu), Tokyo, 1940, vol. 2, pp. 734–5.
15 N. Wakayama, *Jiyu Koeki Anasagashi* (Errors of Free Trade Detected), Tokyo, 1877, Preface; *Wakayama Norikazu Zenshu*, vol. 2, pp. 769–96.
16 *Meiroku Zasshi*, no. 24, 1874; *MBZ*, vol. 18, pp. 172–5.
17 *Minkan Zasshi*, no. 24, 1875; *MBZ*, vol. 10, pp. 307–9.
18 *Meiroku Zasshi*, no. 29, 1875; *MBZ*, vol. 18, pp. 194–6.
19 *Tokai Keizai Shinpo*, no. 1, 1880, editorial.
20 *Tokyo Keizai Zasshi*, no. 706, 1888; *Teiken Taguchi Ukichi Zenshu* (Complete Works of Taguchi Ukichi: hereafter *TUZ*), Tokyo, 1927–9, vol. 4, pp. 458–9.
21 S. Oshima, *Joseiron* (On the Present Situation), Tokyo, 1891, pp. 142–6.
22 *Tokyo Keizai Zasshi*, no. 438, 1888; *TUZ*, vol. 3, pp. 274–7.
23 *Kokka Gakkai Zasshi*, vol. 2, no. 13, 1888; *MBZ*, 1929, vol. 21, pp. 465–9.
24 *Hogaku Kyokai Zasshi*, vol. 10, no. 11, 1892; *MBZ*, vol. 21, pp. 480–4.
25 *Hogaku Kyokai Zasshi*,, vol. 10, no. 12, 1892; vol. 11, nos 1–2, 1893; *MBZ*, vol. 21, pp. 484–92.
26 *Kokka Gakkai Zasshi*, vol. 13, no. 150, 1899.
27 *Tokyo Keizai Zasshi*, nos 1082–91, 1901; *TUZ*, vol. 2, p. 549.
28 M. Toyohara, *Shihon to Rodo no Chowa* (Harmony between Capital and Labour), Tokyo, 1899, pp. 17–25.
29 K. Kuwata, *Oshu Rodo Mondai no Taisei* (Outline of Labour Problems in Europe), Tokyo, 1899, pp. 178–91.
30 Ibid.
31 *Ten Chi Jin* (Heaven, Earth, Humanity), no. 26, 1899.

32 S. Ishikawa and D. Kotoku (eds) 'Nihon Shakaishugishi' (History of Socialism in Japan), *Heimin Shinbun* (Commoners' Newspaper), nos 2–57, Tokyo, 1907; *MBZ*, vol. 21, pp. 361–2.
33 S. Katayama and K. Nishikawa, *Nihon no Rodo Undo* (Labour Movement in Japan), Tokyo, 1901; *MBZ*, vol. 21, pp. 279–80.
34 *MBZ*, vol. 21, pp. 530–7.
35 Reproduced in *Tokyo Keizai Zasshi*, no. 1089, 1901.
36 H. Kawakami, *Shakaishugi Hyoron* (Socialist Review), Tokyo, 1906, pp. 65–7.
37 This is a free translation of 'Chian Keisatsuho', and should not be confused with the notorious 'Chian Ijiho', i.e. Peace Maintenance Act of 1925.
38 E. Sumiya, *Nihon Keizaigakushi* (History of Economic Thought in Japan), Kyoto, 1958, revised 1967, p. 253.

2 THE ECONOMIC THOUGHT OF NISHI AMANE

1 *Meiroku Zasshi* (Meiji Six Journal), no. 1, March 1874; *Meiji Bunka Zenshu* (Collected Works of Meiji Culture), Toyko, vol. 5, p. 51.
2 *Nishi Amane Zenshu* (Complete Works of Nishi Amane: hereafter *NAZ*), Tokyo, 1960–81, vol. 1, p. 170.
3 Ibid., vol. 1, pp. 278–89.
4 Ibid., vol. 1, pp. 282–4.
5 Ibid., vol. 1, pp. 514–55.
6 Ibid., vol. 1, pp. 528–9.
7 Ibid., vol. 1, pp. 532–3.
8 Ibid., vol. 4, p. 235. Strictly speaking, what 'Hyakugaku Renkan' really was cannot be known. All that is left is Nishi's own 'Memorandum', which gives only the title of each part or chapter of the lectures, and a lecture note faithfully taken by a pupil of his by the name of Nagami Yutaka.
9 *NAZ*, vol. 4, pp. 247–50.
10 Irene Hasenburg Butter, *Academic Economics in Holland 1800–1870*, The Hague, 1969, pp. 145–7.
11 *NAZ*, vol. 4, pp. 248–51.
12 Ibid., vol. 3, p. 254.
13 Ibid., vol. 3, pp. 254–5.
14 Ibid., vol. 3, pp. 257–8.
15 *Meiroku Zasshi*, no. 26, 1875; *Fukuzawa Yukichi Zenshu* (Complete Works of Fukuzawa Yukichi), Tokyo, 1958–63, vol. 19, pp. 542–7.
16 *NAZ*, vol. 2, pp. 420–9.

3 THE ECONOMIC THOUGHT OF TSUDA MAMICHI

1 *Meiroku Zasshi* (Meiji Six Journal), no. 8, May 1874; *Meiji Bunka Zenshu* (Collected Works of Meiji Culture: hereafter *MBZ*), Tokyo, vol. 5, 1927, p. 93.
2 *Meiroku Zasshi*, no. 14, July 1874; *MBZ*, vol. 5, p. 126.

3 *Meiroku Zasshi*, no. 35, April 1875; *MBZ*, vol. 5, p. 226.
4 *Tokyo Gakushikaiin Zasshi* (Journal of Tokyo Academy), vol. 15, no. 3, March 1893; vol. 22, no. 5, May 1900.
5 *Meiroku Zasshi*, no. 3, March 1874; *MBZ*, vol. 5, p. 66.
6 Ibid.
7 *Meiroku Zasshi*, nos 4–7, 12, March 1874; *MBZ*, vol. 5, pp. 70–1, 74–5, 80–1, 100–2, 113–14.
8 *Meiroku Zasshi*, no. 6, March 1874; *MBZ*, vol. 5, pp. 82–5.
9 Ibid.
10 *Meiroku Zasshi*, no. 20, November 1874; MBZ, vol. 5, p. 152.
11 *Meiroku Zasshi*, no. 7, May 1874; *MBZ*, vol. 5, p. 91.
12 *Meiroku Zasshi*, no. 24, December 1874; *MBZ*, vol. 5, pp. 171–2.
13 *Meiroku Zasshi*, no. 30, February 1875; *MBZ*, vol. 5, p. 200.
14 *Meiroku Zasshi*, no. 11, June 1874; *MBZ*, vol. 5, pp. 108–10.
15 *Meiroku Zasshi*, no. 9, June 1874; *MBZ*, vol. 5, pp. 98–9.
16 *Meiroku Zasshi*, no. 5, March 1874; *MBZ*, vol. 5, pp. 72–4.
17 *Meiroku Zasshi*, no. 24, December 1874; *MBZ*, vol. 5, pp. 171–2.
18 *Minkan Zasshi* (Popular Magazine), no. 10, February 1875; *MBZ*, vol. 5, pp. 307–9.
19 *Meiroku Zasshi*, no. 34, April 1875; *MBZ*, vol. 5, pp. 221–2.
20 Ibid.
21 See Irene Hasenburg Butter, *Academic Economics in Holland 1800–1870*, The Hague, 1969, pp. 122–6, 145–7.

4 THE ECONOMIC THOUGHT OF FUKUZAWA YUKICHI

1 *Fukuzawa Bunshu* (Works of Fukuzawa), Tokyo, 1875; *Fukuzawa Yukichi Zenshu* (Complete Works of Fukuzawa Yukichi: hereafter *FYZ*), Tokyo, 1958–64, vol. 4, p. 477.
2 See Chapter 1, note 5.
3 See Chapter 1, note 4.
4 *FYZ*, vol. 1, p. 286.
5 *Chambers's Educational Course: Political Economy for Use in Schools and for Private Instruction*, London and Edinburgh, 1873 edn, p. 10.
6 Ibid., p. 12.
7 Ibid., p. 63.
8 Ibid., pp. 13–14.
9 Ibid., p. 49.
10 Ibid., p. 51.
11 Ibid., p. 38.
12 *FYZ*, vol. 3, p. 29.
13 Ibid., vol. 1, p. 392.
14 Ibid., vol. 3, p. 42.
15 Ibid., vol. 3, p. 44.
16 Ibid., vol. 3, p. 92.
17 Ibid., vol. 3, pp. 93–4.
18 Ibid., vol. 4, p. 19.

19 Ibid., vol. 4, p. 207.
20 Ibid., vol. 3, p. 107.
21 Ibid., vol. 3, p. 124.
22 Ibid., vol. 20, p. 53.
23 Ibid., vol. 3, p. 13.
24 Ibid., vol. 19, p. 388.
25 Ibid., vol. 3, pp. 36–7.
26 Ibid., vol. 3, p. 81.
27 Ibid., vol. 3, p. 111.
28 Ibid., vol. 3, pp. 32–3.
29 Ibid., vol. 4, p. 603.
30 Ibid.
31 Ibid., vol. 4, p. 608.
32 Ibid., vol. 4, p. 661.
33 Ibid., vol. 5, p. 167.
34 Ibid., vol. 4, p. 262.
35 Ibid., vol. 4, pp. 289–90.
36 Ibid., vol. 4, p. 290.
37 Ibid., vol. 4, p. 373.
38 For Taguchi's view on railways, see *Tokyo Keizai Zasshi* (The Tokyo Economist), nos 58 and 60 (5 and 25 April 1881).
39 *FYZ*, vol. 4, p. 373.
40 Ibid., vol. 4, pp. 186–7.
41 Ibid., vol. 4, p. 108.
42 Ibid., vol. 4, p. 167.
43 Ibid., vol. 4, p. 107.
44 Ibid., vol. 4, p. 191.
45 Ibid., vol. 4, p. 190.
46 Ibid., vol. 20, p. 24.
47 Ibid., vol. 20, p. 53.
48 Ibid., vol. 20, pp. 123–4. See also Chapter 5, note 11.
49 Ibid., vol. 19, pp. 539–43.
50 Ibid., vol. 20, pp. 146–9.
51 Ibid., vol. 4, pp. 193–4.
52 Ibid., vol. 19, pp. 706–7.
53 For Nishi's and Tsuda's defence of foreigners being allowed to reside and travel anywhere at will, and Fukuzawa's refutation, see Chapters 2 and 3.
54 *FYZ*, vol. 19, pp. 522–4.
55 Ibid., vol. 19, pp. 521–2.
56 Ibid., vol. 19, p. 518.
57 Ibid.
58 Francis Wayland, *The Elements of Political Economy*, New York, 1837, p. 186.
59 *FYZ*, vol. 19, p. 519.
60 Ibid.
61 Ibid., vol. 19, pp. 520–1.
62 Ibid., vol. 4, p. 435.
63 Ibid., vol. 4, p. 632.
64 Ibid., vol. 5, pp. 107–8.

65 Ibid., vol. 4, p. 204.
66 Ibid., vol. 5, p. 108.
67 Ibid., vol. 5, p. 109.
68 Ibid., vol. 5, p. 111.
69 Ibid., vol. 5, pp. 111–12.
70 Ibid., vol. 3, pp. 19–20.
71 Ibid., vol. 4, pp. 268–9.
72 Ibid., vol. 4, p. 258.
73 Ibid., vol. 4, pp. 272–3.
74 Ibid., vol. 4, pp. 270–1.
75 Ibid., vol. 4, pp. 333–4.
76 Ibid., vol. 4, pp. 376–7.
77 Ibid., vol. 4, p. 377.
78 Ibid., vol. 4, p. 122.
79 Ibid., vol. 19, p. 634.
80 Ibid., vol. 4, p. 489.

5 THE BIRTH OF BUSINESS EDUCATION

1 *Kokumin no Tomo* (Friend of the Nation), vol. 14, no. 42, 22 February 1889.
2 Ivan P. Hall, *Mori Arinori*, Cambridge, Mass., 1973, pp. 289–90, 316–17.
3 *Mori Arinori Zenshu* (Complete Works of Mori Arinori), vol. 3, Tokyo, 1972, p. 272.
4 Ibid., p. 334.
5 Ibid., p. 386.
6 Ibid., pp. 336–8.
7 Ibid., p. 334.
8 Ibid., p. 352.
9 Ibid., pp. 363–5.
10 Ibid., p. 17.
11 *Fukuzawa Yukichi Zenshu* (Complete Works of Fukuzawa Yukichi: hereafter *FYZ*), Tokyo, 1958–63, vol. 20, p. 123.
12 Ibid., vol. 3, pp. 333–4.
13 Tomita, it seems, was well liked by the Whitneys. Mrs Whitney was willing to teach him English. It is possible that this friendship led to the decision by Dr Whitney to accept the offer of a job in Japan. The Ambassador, Mori, who was responsible for the Japanese residents in America, also trusted and liked Tomita and recommended him as a guide and interpreter when the so-called Iwakura Mission (see Chapter 9, note 12) arrived in Washington in 1872. It was Iwakura Tomomi who made Tomita acting Consul in New York.
14 It may be of interest in a historical context that the translator of Carey's book, Inukai Tsuyoshi, eventually became Prime Minister and was assassinated at the time of a nationalist or militarist coup (1932) in what is known as the 'May the Fifteenth Incident'.
15 *Mori Arinori Zenshu*, vol. 1, 1972, p. 323. See also *FYZ*, vol. 17, pp. 186–7.
16 *Katsu Kaishu Zenshu* (Complete Works of Katsu Kaishu, i.e. Rintaro),

Tokyo, 1973, vol. 1, p. 30. See also Clara Whitney, *Clara's Diary*, Tokyo, 1979, pp. 36–7.

17 *Mori Arinori Zenshu*, vol. 1, pp. 319–20.

18 For further information on the developments in curricula during the earliest days of the school, see C. Sugiyama and H. Mizuta (eds) *Enlightenment and Beyond: Political Economy comes to Japan*, Tokyo, 1988, pp. 157–8.

19 *Shoho Koshujo* (Commercial Training School), document kept in Tokyo Prefectural Record Office, pp. 62–3.

20 For the subjects to be taught, see C. Sugiyama and H. Mizuta, (eds) op. cit., pp. 158–9.

21 For the earliest days of the LSE, see, for example, Janet Beveridge, *An Epic of Clare Market: Birth and Early Days of the London School of Economics*, London, 1960, pp. 14–41.

22 Among Ashley's related works are: *Commercial Education*, London, 1926; *Business Economics*, London and New York, 1926.

6 THE BIRTH OF A LIMITED COMPANY

1 *Maruzen Hyakunenshi* (A Hundred Years of Maruzen and Co.), 1980–1, vol. 1, pp. 30–1.

2 *Fukuzawa Yukichi Zenshu* (Complete Works of Fukuzawa Yukichi), Tokyo, 1958–64, vol. 17, p. 133.

3 *Maruzen Hyakunenshi*, vol. 1, pp. 150–1.

4 *Tokyo Shoko Hakuran'e* (Illustrated Views of Trade and Industry in Tokyo): see *Maruzen Hyakunenshi*, vol. 1, pp. 236–9.

5 Though dated 1869, what exists is only a later version reproduced in 1874, the original version having been lost because of the fire at Nihonbashi.

6 *Maruzen Hyakunenshi*, vol. 1, p. 40.

7 Ibid., p. 49.

8 See also Chapter 4, esp. note 46.

9 See Chapter 4 and Chapter 1, note 5.

10 It is worth mentioning that the concept of a limited company in a clearer and more explicit form was introduced only two years later, in 1871, by Shibusawa Eiichi, who, incidentally, occupies a notable position in the modern history of Japan as a result of his successful economic activities allied to his devout adherence to the traditional Confucian moral codes that such figures as Nishi and Fukuzawa rejected as vain learning.

In *Tachiai Ryakusoku* (Summary Rules of Companies), which he wrote when he was a young government official at the Ministry of Finance and had the Ministry publish, he says that he absorbed necessary information on commercial practice and laws while he stayed in France for about a year and a half as one of the attendants dispatched by the Shogunate government to the World Exhibition held in Paris. According to his text, in order to run a firm successfully, regardless of the kind of business, it is necessary to decide in advance the required amount of capital, which should be composed of stocks held by those who want to join. Profit or loss should be distributed to those stockholders in proportion to the sum of their stocks.

The pervasive spirit of nationalism is evident here too. On the one hand, the text states that firms are independent of the government, and so the government should not decree what they must do. On the other hand, it maintains that those who combine themselves in firms, although pursuing their own interest, nevertheless carry out the circulation and distribution of goods for society, and so should keep the public interest in mind; that the essential task of commerce is to pursue and realize the public interest of all of Japan; and that it would bring disgrace not only upon the firms themselves but also upon the whole nation if they were to act in such an unlawful way as to be despised by foreign merchants.

7 THE BIRTH OF ECONOMIC JOURNALISM

1 The Academy was not merely an institution for military training. Among other subjects to be taught were logic, ethics, French, English, mathematics, astronomy and natural history. The Academy, which had been established by the former Shogun who was now a mere lord of the Shizuoka clan, was absorbed after only three years by the Military School that was established in Tokyo by the new government.
2 *Teiken Taguchi Ukichi Zenshu* (Complete Works of Taguchi Ukichi), Tokyo, 1927–9, vol. 3, p. 25.
3 Ibid., vol. 3, pp. 52–64.
4 Ibid., vol. 3, pp. 22–4.
5 Ibid.
6 Alexander Allen Shand (1844[?]–1930) stayed in Japan from 1863 to 1874.
7 *Tokyo Keizai Zasshi* (hereafter *TKZ*), no. 1, 29 January 1879.
8 *Tokai Keizai Shinpo* (hereafter *TKS*), no. 1, 21 August 1880.
9 *TKZ*, no. 37, 5 September 1880.
10 Ibid.
11 *TKS*, no. 3, 15 September 1880.
12 *TKZ*, no. 38, 15 September 1880.
13 *TKZ*, no. 39, 25 September 1880.
14 *TKS*, no. 5, 5 October 1880.
15 *TKZ*, no. 41, 15 October 1880.
16 *TKS*, no. 7, 25 October 1880.
17 *TKS*, no. 8, 5 November 1880.
18 *TKS*, no. 9, 15 October 1880.
19 *TKZ*, no. 44, 15 October 1880.
20 *TKZ*, no. 46, 5 December 1880.
21 *TKS*, no. 13, 25 December 1880.
22 *TKS*, no. 17, 15 February 1881.
23 *TKS*, no. 18, 25 February 1881.
24 *TKS*, no. 20, 15 March 1881.
25 *TKS*, no. 21, 25 March 1881.
26 *TKZ*, no. 57, 25 March 1881.
27 *TKZ*, no. 59, 15 April 1881.

8 PROTECTIONISTS ON THE OFFENSIVE

1 *Wakayama Norikazu Zenshu* (Complete Works of Wakayama Norikazu), Tokyo, 1940, vol. 2, p. 772.
2 Ibid.
3 Ibid., pp. 759–60.
4 Ibid., pp. 760–1.
5 Ibid., p. 769.
6 Ibid., pp. 771–4.
7 Ibid., p. 794.
8 Ibid., pp. 735–6.
9 Ibid., pp. 737–9.
10 *Minkan Zasshi*, no. 10, February 1875; *Meiji Bunka Zenshu* (Collected Works of Meiji Culture: hereafter *MBZ*), Tokyo vol. 5, p. 309.
11 *Meiroku Zasshi* (Meiji Six Journal), no. 29, 1875; *MBZ*, vol. 18, pp. 194–6.
12 *Joseiron* (On the Present Situation), Tokyo, 1891, p. 142.
13 Ibid., p. 144.
14 Ibid., pp. 145–6.

9 THE IMPERIAL CONSTITUTION

1 *Fukuzawa Yukichi Zenshu* (Complete Works of Fukuzawa Yukichi), Tokyo, vol. 1, pp. 28–9.
2 *Meiji Bunka Zenshu* (Collected Works of Meiji Culture: hereafter *MBZ*), Tokyo, 1928, vol. 13, pp. 88–9.
3 Masatsugu Inada, *Meiji Kenpo Seiritsushi* (History of the Birth of the Meiji Constitution), Tokyo, 1960–2, vol. 1, *passim*.
4 *Meiroku Zasshi* (Meiji Six Journal), no. 4, 1874; *MBZ*, vol. 5, pp. 69–70.
5 *Meiroku Zasshi*, nos 3, 29; *MBZ*, vol. 5, pp. 66–7, 193–4; *Nishi Amane Zenshu* (Complete Works of Nishi Amane), Tokyo, 1961, vol. 2, pp. 238–40, 242–5.
6 *Meiroku Zasshi*, no. 3; *MBZ*, vol. 5, pp. 62–3; *Mori Arinori Zenshi* (Complete Works of Mori Arinori), vol. 1, Tokyo, 1966, pp. 16–17.
7 'The Japanese Ambassador on Public Affairs: An Interview on his Departure from England', *Pall Mall Gazette*, London, 26 February 1884.
8 Athenaeum Club on Pall Mall, of which Mori was a fellow member.
See Chapter 5, note 2; the author quotes (p. 317) the letter that Spencer wrote much later, in August 1892, to Kaneko Kentaro, which says: 'When Mori, the then Japanese ambassador, submitted to me his draft for a Japanese constitution, I gave him very conservative advice, contending that it was impossible that the Japanese, hitherto accustomed to despotic rule, should all at once become capable of constitutional government.'
9 Shigeki Nishimura, *Seitai Sanshuron* (Three Types of Political System), Tokyo, 1875.
10 Inada, op. cit., vol. 1, pp. 331–3.
11 See Ito's letter to Iwakura, dated 21 December 1879, in Kentaro Kaneko (ed.) *Ito Hirobumi Den* (Life of Ito Hirobumi), Tokyo, 1940, vol. 2, pp. 188–9.

12 Shoichi Tanaka, *Iwakura Shisetsu Dan* (Iwakura Mission), Tokyo, 1978, pp. 138, 193.
13 *Inoue Kowashi Den: Shiryohen* (Life of Inoue Kowashi: Volumes of Papers), Tokyo, 1966, vol. 1, *passim*. See also J. Pittau, *Political Thought in Early Meiji Japan*, Cambridge, Mass., 1967, pp. 165–77.
14 See, for example, G. Akita, *Foundations of Constitutional Government in Modern Japan 1868–1900*, Cambridge, Mass., 1967, pp. 31–57.
15 *Inoue Kowashi Den: Shiryohen*, vol. 1, pp. 47–54.
16 Document kept in Kokugakuin University, Tokyo.
17 For Roesler's role see, for example, J. Siemes, *Hermann Roesler and the Making of the Meiji State, with his Commentaries on the Meiji Constitution*, Tokyo, 1966, pp. 18ff.
18 *Nakae Chomin Zenshu* (Complete Works of Nakae Chomin), Tokyo, 1983, vol. 10, pp. 79–123.

APPENDIX
ENLIGHTENMENT BY TRANSLATION

1 *Fukuzawa Yukichi Zenshu* (Complete Works of Fukuzawa Yukichi: hereafter *FYZ*), Tokyo, 1958–63, vol. 7, p. 169.
2 Ibid., vol. 1, p. 385.
3 Ibid., vol. 1, p. 386.
4 Ibid., vol. 2, p. 115.
5 Ibid., vol. 1, p. 23.
6 H. B. Bryant and H. D. Stratton, and S. S. Packard, *Bryant and Stratton's Common School Bookkeeping: Embracing Single and Double Entry*, New York and Chicago, 1861, p. 11.
7 *FYZ*, vol. 3, pp. 333–4.
8 Ibid., vol. 3, pp. 334–5.
9 Ibid.
10 Ibid., vol. 3, p. 30.
11 Ibid., vol. 2, p. 237.
12 Clara Whitney, *Clara's Diary*, Tokyo, 1979, p. 165.
13 Ibid., p. 270.
14 Ibid., p. 221.
15 *FYZ*, vol. 20, p. 37.
16 Ibid., vol. 1, pp. 22–3.
17 Ibid.

BIBLIOGRAPHY

Akita, G. *Foundations of Constitutional Government in Modern Japan 1868–1990*, Cambridge, Mass., 1967.
Amano, T. *Keizai Genron* (Principles of Political Economy), Tokyo, 1886.
Amano, T. *Shosei Hyojun* (Principles of Commercial Policy), Tokyo, 1886.
Ashley, Sir W. J. *Business Economics*, London and New York, 1926.
Ashley, Sir W. J. *Commercial Education*, London, 1926.
Bastiat, F. *Sophismes économiques*, Paris, 1845–8.
Beveridge, J. *An Epic of Clare Market: Birth and Early Days of the London School of Economics*, London, 1960.
Blacker, C. *The Japanese Enlightenment: A Study of the Writings of Fukuzawa Yukichi*, Cambridge, 1964.
Bluntchli, J. C. (trans.) *Kokuho Hanron* (General Theory of Law), Tokyo, 1872.
Bryant, H. B. and Stratton, H. D. *Bryant and Stratton's Common School Book-Keeping: Embracing Single and Double Entry*, New York and Chicago, 1861.
[Burton, J. H.] *Chambers's Educational Course: Political Economy, for Use in Schools, and for Private Instruction*, London and Edinburgh, 1852.
Butter, I. H. *Academic Economics in Holland 1800–1870*, The Hague, 1969.
Byles, J. B. *Sophisms of Free Trade and Popular Political Economy Examined*, London, 1849.
Cairnes, J. E. *The Character and Logical Method of Political Economy*, London, 1857.
Carey, H. C. *Principles of Social Science*, Philadelphia and London, 1858–9.
Ellis, W. *Outlines of Social Economy*, London, 1846.
Fawcett, H. *Manual of Political Economy*, London, 1863.
Fawcett, M. G. *Political Economy for Beginners*, London, 1870.
Fukuzawa, Y. 'Ajia Shokoku to no Wasen' (Peace or War with Asian Countries), *Yubihnochi*, 7 October 1875.
Fukuzawa, Y. 'Boeki Shokai Kaigyo no Enzetsu' (Opening Speech of a Trading Company), Tokyo, 1880.
Fukuzawa, Y. *Bunkenron* (Decentralization of Power), Tokyo, 1877.
Fukuzawa, Y. *Bunmeiron no Gairyaku* (An Outline of a Theory of Civilization), Tokyo, 1875.

Fukuzawa, Y. *Choai no Ho* (A Guide to Bookkeeping), Tokyo, 1875.
Fukuzawa, Y. *Domo Oshiegusa* (A Reader for the Infant), Tokyo, 1872.
Fukuzawa, Y. *Fukuo Jiden* (Fukuzawa's Autobiography), Tokyo, 1899.
Fukuzawa, Y. *Fukuzawa Bunshu* (Works of Fukuzawa), Tokyo, 1875–9.
Fukuzawa, Y. 'Gaikokujin no Naichi Zakkyo o yurusu bekarazaru no Ron' (Foreigners should not be allowed to live freely among the Japanese), *Meiroku Zasshi*, no. 26, 1875.
Fukuzawa, Y. *Gakumon no Susume* (An Encouragement of Learning), Tokyo, 1872–4.
Fukuzawa, Y. *Jiji Shogen* (Current Affairs Briefly Discussed), Tokyo, 1881.
Fukuzawa, Y. *Keimo Tenarai no Bun* (Enlightening Penmanship), Tokyo, 1871.
Fukuzawa, Y. 'Maruya Shosha no Ki' (Prospectus of Maruya & Co.), 1869.
Fukuzawa, Y. *Minkan Keizairoku* (Popular Political Economy), Tokyo, 1878–81.
Fukuzawa, Y. 'Nakatsu Rubetsu no Sho' (Farewell to Nakatsu), Tokyo, 1870.
Fukuzawa, Y. 'Seitai Wagi no Enzetsu' (Speech on the Peace of Taiwan), *Meiroku Zasshi*, no. 21, 1874.
Fukuzawa, Y. *Seiyo Jijo* (Conditions in the West), Tokyo, 1866–70.
Fukuzawa, Y. *Seiyo Ryoko Annai* (A Guide to Western Trips), Tokyo, 1867.
Fukuzawa, Y. 'Shogakko o tatsuru no Shui' (Prospectus of the School of Commerce), 1875.
Fukuzawa, Y. 'Tojin Orai' (Foreigners In and Out), n.d. (*c.* 1865).
Fukuzawa, Y. *Tsuzoku Kokkenron* (Popular Theory of the State's Rights), Tokyo, 1878.
Fukuzawa, Y. *Tsuzoku Minkenron* (Popular Theory of People's Rights), Tokyo, 1878.
Fukuzawa Yukichi Zenshu (Complete Works of Fukuzawa Yukichi), Tokyo, 1958–63.
Hall, I. P. *Mori Arinori*, Cambridge, Mass., 1970.
Havens, R. H. *Nishi Amane and Modern Japanese Thought*, Princeton, 1970.
Hayashi, M. *Keizai Benmo* (Economic Misunderstanding Corrected), Tokyo, 1878.
Heimin Shinbun (Commoners' Newspaper), nos. 2–57, Tokyo, 1907.
Honjo, E. *Nihon Keizai Shisoshi* (History of Economic Thought in Japan), Tokyo, 1966.
Inada, M. *Meiji Kenpo Seiritsushi* (History of the Birth of the Meiji Constitution), Tokyo, 1960–2.
Inoue Kowashi Den: Shiryohen (Life of Inoue Kowashi: Volumes of Papers), Tokyo, 1966.
Jevons, W. S. *Money and Mechanism of Exchange*, London, 1875.
Kanda, T. *Denzei Shinpo* (New Land Tax Proposed), Tokyo, 1872.
Kanda, T. *No-Sho Ben* (On Agriculture and Trade), Tokyo, 1861.
Kaneko, K. (ed.) *Ito Hirobumi Den* (Life of Ito Hirobumi), Tokyo, 1940.
Katayama, S. and Nishikawa, K. *Nihon no Rodo Undo* (Labour Movement in Japan), Tokyo, 1901.
Kato, H. *Koeki Mondo* (A Dialogue on Trade), Tokyo, 1869.
Kawakami, H. *Shakaishugi Hyoron* (Socialist Review), Tokyo, 1906.

Kokka Gakkai Zasshi (Bulletin of the Society for the Study of the State), vol. 13, Tokyo, 1899.
Kokumin no Tomo (Friend of the Nation), vol. 14, Tokyo, 1889.
Kuwata, K. *Oshu Rodo Mondai no Taisei* (Outline of Labour Problems in Europe), Tokyo, 1899.
List, F. *Das nationale System der politischen Oekonomie*, Stuttgart and Tübingen, 1841.
Malthus, T. R. *An Essay on the Principle of Population*, London, 1798.
'Maruya Shosha no Ki' (Prospectus of Maruya & Co.), 1869.
Maruzen Hyakunenshi (A Hundred Years of Maruzen & Co.), Tokyo, 1980–1.
Meiji Bunka Zenshu (Collected Works of Meiji Culture), vols 5, 9, 15, 18, Tokyo, 1928–30.
Meiroku Zasshi (Meiji Six Journal), nos 3, 4, 5, 8, 24, 26, 29, 34, Tokyo, 1874–5.
Mill, J. S. *Principles of Political Economy*, London, 1848.
Mill, J. S. *Utilitarianism*, London, 1863.
Minkan Zasshi (Popular Magazine), nos 10, 24, Tokyo, 1875.
Mori, A. *Education in Japan*, Washington, 1873.
Mori, A. 'Kyoshu' (On Religious Belief), *Meiroku Zasshi*, no. 6, 1874.
Mori Arinori Zenshu (Complete Works of Mori Arinori), vols 1, 3, Tokyo, 1972.
Nakae, C. *Nakae Chomin Zenshu* (Complete Works of Nakae Chomin), vol. 10, Tokyo, 1983.
Nishi, A. 'Hyakugaku Renkan' (All Learnings Combined), n.d.
Nishi, A. *Hyakuichi Shinron* (Uniformity of All Learnings Reviewed), Tokyo, 1874.
Nishi, A. 'Jinsei Sanbosetsu' (Three Treasures of Life), *Meiroku Zasshi*, nos 38, 39, 40, 42, etc., Tokyo, 1874.
Nishi, A. 'Kyomonron' (On Religious Sects), *Meiroku Zasshi*, no. 4 *et al.*, Tokyo, 1874. *Nishi Amane Zenshu* (Complete Works of Nishi Amane), vols 1, 2, Tokyo, 1960–81.
Nishimura, S. *Seitai Sanshuron* (Three Types of Political System), Tokyo, 1875.
Onna Daigaku (Great Learnings for Women), n.d.
Oshima, S. *Joseiron* (On the Present Situation), Tokyo, 1891.
Pall Mall Gazette, London, February 1884.
Perry, A. L. *Elements of Political Economy*, New York, 1866.
Pittau, J. *Political Thought in Early Meiji Japan*, Cambridge, Mass., 1967.
Sada, K. *Saibai Keizairon* (On Cultivating the Economy), Tokyo, 1878.
Say, J. B. *Traité d'Economie Politique*, Paris, 1803.
Shibusawa, E. *Tachiai Ryakusoku* (Summary Rules of Companies), Tokyo, 1871.
'Shogakko o tatsuru no Shui' (Reason for Establishing a Commercial School), 1875.
Shoho Koshujo (Commercial Training School), Tokyo, n.d.
Siemes, J. *Hermann Roesler and the Making of the Meiji State, with his Commentaries on the Meiji Constitution*, Tokyo, 1966.
Smith, A. *An Inquiry into the Nature and Causes of the Wealth of Nations*, London, 1776.

Sugiyama, C. and Mizuta, H. (eds) *Enlightenment and Beyond: Political Economy comes to Japan*, Tokyo, 1988.
Sumiya, E. *Nihon Keizaigakushi* (History of Economic Thought in Japan), Kyoto, 1967.
Taguchi, U. *Jiyu Koeki Nihon Keizairon* (On the Free Trade Japanese Economy), Tokyo, 1878.
Teiken Taguchi Ukichi Zenshu (Complete Works of Taguchi Ukichi), Tokyo, 1927–9.
Tanaka, S. *Iwakura Shisetsu Dan* (Iwakura Mission), Tokyo, 1978.
Ten Chi Jin (Heaven, Earth, Humanity), no. 26, 1899.
Tokai Keizai Shinpo (Tokai New Economic Review), Tokyo, 1880–1.
Tokyo Gakushikaiin Zasshi (Journal of Tokyo Academy), vols 15, 22, Tokyo, 1893, 1900.
Tokyo Keizai Zasshi (The Tokyo Economist), nos 1, 3, 5, 7, 8, 37, 38, 41, 44, 58–60, 437, 706, 1082–91, Tokyo, 1879–1901.
Toyohara, M. *Shihon to Rodo no Chowa* (Harmony between Capital and Labour), Tokyo, 1899.
Tsuda, M. 'Boeki Kenkoron' (On the Balance of Trade), *Meiroku Zasshi*, no. 26, Tokyo, 1875.
Tsuda, M. 'Fufu Dokenben' (On the Equal Rights of Husband and Wife), *Meiroku Zasshi*, no. 35, Tokyo, 1875.
Tsuda, M. 'Fukushoron' (On Official Insignia), *Meiroku Zasshi*, no. 8, Tokyo, 1874.
Tsuda, M. 'Hogozei o Hi to suru Setsu' (Protective Duties Criticized), *Meiroku Zasshi*, no. 5, Tokyo, 1874.
Tsuda, M. 'Jinzairon' (People of Talent), *Meiroku Zasshi*, no. 30, Tokyo, 1875.
Tsuda, M. 'Kaisetsu' (On Ghosts), *Meiroku Zasshi*, no. 25, Tokyo, 1874.
Tsuda, M. 'Seiron' (On Government), *Meiroku Zasshi*, no. 12, Tokyo, 1874.
Tsuda, M. *Taisei Kokuhoron* (On the Laws in the West), 1868.
Tsuda, M. 'Tengusetsu' (On Long-nosed Goblins), *Meiroku Zasshi*, no. 14, Tokyo, 1874.
Tsuda, M. 'Unsoron' (On Transportation), *Meiroku Zasshi*, no. 9, Tokyo, 1874.
Vissering, S. *Handboek van Praktische Staathuishoudkunde*, Amsterdam, 1860–5.
Wakayama, N. *Hogozeisetsu* (On Protective Duties), Tokyo, 1871.
Wakayama, N. *Jiyu Koeki Anasagashi* (Errors of Free Trade Detected), Tokyo, 1877.
Wakayama Norikazu Zenshu (Complete Works of Wakayama Norikazu), vols 1, 2, Tokyo, 1940.
Walker, F. A. *Science of Wealth*, New York, 1866.
Wayland, F. *The Elements of Moral Science*, New York, 1844.
Wayland, F. *The Elements of Political Economy*, New York, 1837.
Whitney, C. *Clara's Diary*, Tokyo, 1979.

INDEX